BIG
ISSUES

First published in 2015 by Elevation for Spring Harvest

Elevation is part of Memralife Group, registered charity number 1126997, a company limited by guarantee, registered in England and Wales, number 6667924.

14 Horsted Square, Uckfield, East Sussex, TN22 1QG

The right of Spring Harvest to be identified as the Author of this Work has been asserted by him in accordance with Copyright, Designs and Patents Act 1988

British Library Cataloguing in Publication Data

All Scripture quotations unless indicated otherwise taken from the THE HOLY BIBLE, NEW INTERNATIONAL VERSION®, NIV® Copyright © 1973, 1978, 1984, 2011 by Biblica, Inc.® Used by permission. All rights reserved worldwide.

A catalogue record for this book is available from the British Library

ISBN 978-1-899788-99-6

Credits:

Writers: Jay Butcher, Care For The Family, Gemma Dunning, Ali Ellsmore, Paul Flavel, Ems Hancock, Ian Henderson, Steve Holloway, Pauline Horder, Liz Massey, Mark Massey, Paul Oxley, Ruth Perrett, Kiera Phyo, Restored Relationships, Robin Rolls, Romance Academy, Jason Royce, Chris Simpkins, Helen Warnock, Paul Weston

Design by: Ascent Creative
Project Coordinators: Steph Adam, Jaqs Graham
Printed by Halcyon

Contents

1

God and Spiritual Things

New Life

The adventure begins...

Warning: What you are about to read may seriously improve your life.

Maybe you're reading this because someone has been speaking to you about becoming a Christian. That's great! In fact, that's why this was written.

God created the world. The important question here isn't how he did it, but why.

- He created it for people to enjoy.
- He created it perfect, with a purpose and a plan.

God wanted a relationship with us so much that he created us to be perfect like him. He gave us freedom, but we used that freedom to go against him. The result of that rebellion (sin) meant that we became separated from God and the perfect world that he made for us was broken. (Check out Genesis chapters 1-3 at the beginning of the Bible).

God created you. The Bible says that God knew you before you were born and that he formed you in your mother's body (Psalm 139:13). Whatever the circumstances of your birth, you were meant to be here.

- God created you to have a relationship with him.
- God created you perfect, with a purpose and a plan.

God gave us guidelines to show us how to live in relationship with him and each other. You only need to watch the news to see that we have not kept within those instructions and that the whole world suffers the consequences. However good we think we are - we're not perfect. In fact, our failure to live a perfect life has separated us from God. The Bible says that this separation leads to death – not just physically, but spiritually too. (Check out Romans 3:23 and 6:23).

Everyone who has ever lived has rebelled against God - except one...

The only way that God could repair the perfect relationship with us was by sending his Son - Jesus.

Jesus is not a fairytale or a myth. He was a real man and historical evidence shows that he lived and died. The Bible explains why:

- Jesus came to repair our relationship with God.
- Jesus was perfect and came to earth with a purpose and a plan.

He was totally human and faced every difficulty and temptation that we face, but he remained perfect. He was the only one who didn't deserve death and separation from God - yet this is what happened.

His death on the cross was not only gruesome, but it also carried with it the consequences of the guilt and sin of everyone who has ever lived. He took the punishment that you deserve so that you wouldn't have to. 'God made him who had no sin to be sin for us...' 2 Corinthians 5:21.

Just think, Jesus gave up the perfection of heaven to come to earth and die for you. Why would he do that? Because he loves you and he couldn't love you any more than that.

And there's more. After Jesus died on the cross, he was buried in the grave. But three days later, he came back to life again. Risen from the dead. Really alive. (You can read the story in Luke 24.) Death now has a human shaped hole in it – that is – Jesus showed us that he has power to overcome death, and when we follow him, we can live beyond death.

'But God demonstrates his own love for us in this: While we were still sinners, Christ died for us.'
Romans 5:8.

If Jesus loves us this much, how should we respond?

There was a man in the Bible called Nicodemus who came to see Jesus. Jesus explained to him that he needed to be born again - to have another birth. Nicodemus was spiritually dead and separated from God and he needed to give everything over to Jesus so he could have new life (See John 3:1-21).

You can have the same new life that Nicodemus and millions of others have had. God promises to forgive you and fill you with his Spirit:

- He will give you a new relationship with him that goes on forever, even into a life beyond this one.
- He promises to make you perfect in his eyes and give you a new purpose for your life.

But, before you do this you need to know there is a cost. Being a Christian can be hard. When you give your life to Jesus he wants you to live it for him. That means that sometimes you may have to let go of what you want and do what God wants. There will be occasions when living for Jesus means making difficult decisions and standing out from the crowd.

If you ask God to forgive you for your rebellion and ask him to take control of your life, he promises that he will. The Bible says, 'If we confess our sins, he is faithful and just and will forgive us our sins and purify us from all unrighteousness' (1 John 1:9)

Life is an adventure and the only way to get the best out of it is to become the person Jesus made you to be. When you accept and believe in him you become God's child - a new person (See John 1:12 and 2 Corinthians 5:17). That's what it means to be born again.

If you want to have this rebirth then you might like to use the following prayer. It's important to tell another Christian so they can help you with the rest of the adventure. Ask them about how going to church, reading the Bible and prayer has helped them to grow as a Christian.

> **Jesus**
> **Thank you that you love me just as I am**
> **I know that I have gone my own way**
> **I'm sorry**
> **Thank you for dying on the cross in my place**
> **Please forgive me and fill me with your Holy Spirit**
> **From this point on, I want to live for you alone**
> **Thank you that you will never leave me**
> **Amen**

What does the Bible say?

Psalm 139:13 'For you created my inmost being; you knit me together in my mother's womb.'

Romans 3:23 'For all have sinned and fall short of the glory of God'

Romans 6:23 'For the wages of sin is death, but the gift of God is eternal life in Christ Jesus our Lord.'

2 Corinthians 5:21 'God made him [Jesus] who had no sin to be sin for us, so that in him we might become the righteousness of God.'

Luke 23:34 'Jesus said, "Father, forgive them, for they do not know what they are doing."'

1 John 1:9 'If we confess our sins, he is faithful and just and will forgive us our sins and purify us from all unrighteousness.'

John 1:12 'Yet to all who did receive him, to those who believed in his name, he gave the right to become children of God.'

2 Corinthians 5:17 'Therefore, if anyone is in Christ, the new creation has come: The old has gone, the new is here!'

✚ Where can I get more help?

- Go to page 66-71 for more information and recommended resources.
- Get involved in your local church.
- Get involved with your school or university CU.

Getting Closer To God

What's the issue?

One of the great aspects of being a Christian is we have now entered into a relationship with God. We can be close to God!

As we seek to follow him with our lives we want to keep close to God. This isn't always easy, as sometimes we will find it hard being a Christian - but hold on! Remember God does not stop loving us and even if at times life goes a little 'pear shaped', we simply need to keep coming back to God. Don't lose sight; this is a lifelong following God you have entered into. Take your whole life to enjoy following him and getting to know him more.

What can I do?

Make time to talk to God…. It sounds simple but often it's the simple things we ignore. Talk, share, pray and read the Bible, and do it regularly.

Connect with other Christians and keep having conversations about God with them. Engage in some regular time of corporate worship. Keep committed to a church. We need this company more than we realise.

Keep confessing sin… Just because we are Christians unfortunately doesn't mean we always make the best decisions or do the right things. Be honest with God and allow him to deal with your sin.

Ask for wisdom… Watch out for things that take you away from God and be wise. Ask him to help you make good decisions about your life.

Enjoy sharing your life with him… You have your whole life to walk with God. You will experience many seasons in this, times when God seems very close and present and times when he may seem a little more distant. Don't let this discourage you. Keep your heart set on him and he will be with you. Remember, following God is not based on feelings but faith - he is with us.

What does the Bible say?

James 4:8   'Come near to God and he will come near to you.'

1 John 3:1   'See what great love the Father has lavished on us, that we should be called children of God! And that is what we are!'

Hebrews 10:23-25   'Let us hold unswervingly to the hope we profess, for he who promised is faithful. And let us consider how we may spur one another on toward love and good deeds, not giving up meeting together, as some are in the habit of doing, but encouraging one another - and all the more as you see the Day approaching.'

1 John 1:9   'If we confess our sins, he is faithful and just and will forgive us our sins and purify us from all unrighteousness.'

✚ Where can I get more help?

- Get involved in your local church.
- Connect with your youth group.
- Get involved with your school or university CU.

Courage & Confidence

?! What's the issue?

Sometimes we will find ourselves in situations where we begin to doubt our faith and our God – am I really a Christian? Could God really love me? Am I good enough?

In those times we need to put our hope in God, who does not change his mind about loving us. He does not love us on a Monday and then by Friday decide he doesn't love us any more. He has committed to love us FOREVER. So when you find the doubts creep in, remember who God is and that he is big enough to love you - warts and all.

Another issue that can affect us is when we find ourselves in difficult situations. Maybe you have hard decisions to make because you are a Christian and you are worried it will affect your friendships. Or maybe you are going through a tough time and you simply need God with you in it.

😞 Why me?

Don't think you are alone if you are having doubts or lacking courage. Many people have walked with God before you and faced similar dilemmas.

⚡ What can I do?

In these situations, pick up your Bible and read one of the following stories. These are about ordinary people like us who needed God big time. Take comfort and inspiration from their lives. The same God who was with them is with you.

Joshua 1 As Joshua was about to step into a new position of leadership note how many times God reminds him to be strong and courageous.

Daniel 3:16-18 If you have time, read the rest of chapter 3 as well. These three men didn't bargain with God, they were not saying to God, 'we will serve you if you rescue us', but look at how they were committed to God in both the easy and the hard times. These sentences are so inspiring, the can make us want to walk with God in the easy and the hard times.

Mark 4:35-41 The God you serve has power greater than we can imagine.

What does the Bible say?

Hebrews 10:19-22   'Therefore, brothers and sisters, since we have confidence to enter the Most Holy Place by the blood of Jesus, by a new and living way opened for us through the curtain, that is, his body, and since we have a great priest over the house of God, let us draw near to God with a sincere heart and with the full assurance that faith brings, having our hearts sprinkled to cleanse us from a guilty conscience and having our bodies washed with pure water.'

Where can I get more help?

- Talk to other Christians about what you are going through.
- Find people who can pray with you.
- Memorise helpful scripture and hold onto it.

A Life-Changing Story

?! What's the issue?

Did you know that there is an amazing story unfolding all around us?
Everyone is part of this story but not everybody realises it!
Everybody is affected by this story but many people have never even heard it told!

This life-changing story is the story of God, who is rescuing this broken world and our broken lives through his son, Jesus. It is the story of Jesus showing us how to be the people we were always intended to be.

Our friends desperately need to hear this story!

☹ Why me?

Telling this life-changing story to our friends will normally feel like a pretty scary thing to do. What if they think I'm a weirdo? What if they're not interested? Sometimes, we think it would be a lot easier if God just did this job himself! The thing is, God has never been into just doing it all by himself. Ever since the dawn of time God has asked us to join with him in whatever work he is doing. He wants us to do it all together! So don't worry - God is doing his part, revealing himself in many different ways to everyone around, and he is asking us to shout about him at the same time!

So we can't just leave this job to God, but we can't just leave it to the 'professionals' either. Sometimes we think that people need to hear the story from someone who is standing on a stage or someone who is really funny or someone who lives a totally 'holy' life. Trust me - if they are your friends, the story will make a lot more sense coming from you!

⚡ What can I do?

People need to hear the story, so the easiest thing to do is just tell them. But what if people could actually see this amazing story at work in our lives? What if people could actually see Jesus rescuing our lives? What if people could actually see Jesus rescuing this world? If we say that this story changes lives, what if they could see that our lives were changed?

So as your life changes, tell people why.

As you become more like the person you were made to be; tell people how that happened.

As you join with God in rescuing this world, tell people the story.

What does the Bible say?

The Bible is full of encouragement for us to join with God in telling the story. But just for starters check out:

Exodus 19:3-6   'Then Moses went up to God, and the Lord called to him from the mountain and said, "This is what you are to say to the descendants of Jacob and what you are to tell the people of Israel: 'You yourselves have seen what I did to Egypt, and how I carried you on eagles' wings and brought you to myself. Now if you obey me fully and keep my covenant, then out of all nations you will be my treasured possession. Although the whole earth is mine, you will be for me a kingdom of priests and a holy nation.' These are the words you are to speak to the Israelites".

Matthew 10:7   'As you go, proclaim this message: "The kingdom of heaven has come near."

Matthew 28: 19-20   'Therefore go and make disciples of all nations, baptising them in the name of the Father and of the Son and of the Holy Spirit, and teaching them to obey everything I have commanded you. And surely I am with you always, to the very end of the age.'

1 Peter 2:9   'But you are a chosen people, a royal priesthood, a holy nation, God's special possession, that you may declare the praises of him who called you out of darkness into his wonderful light.'

✛ Where can I get more help?

- Go to page 66-71 for more information and recommended resources.
- Speak to your youth leader who can give you some pointers.

There is no substitute for just jumping in, getting involved and having a go!

Live Life To The Max

> **I have come that they may have life, and have it to the full.**
> Jesus (John 10:10)

Being a Christian isn't always easy. That's the point. Life isn't about getting from it what you can - being as rich or as famous or as popular as you possibly can. But, life is about living. Jesus told us that he came to earth so that we can live life to the max. At times, living life his way is hard work, but it is well worth it. This life we live with Jesus will never end, even when our bodies die, we will continue to live with Jesus, and one day will be reunited with our bodies in the resurrection, so that we can live with Jesus in his eternal kingdom.

Many people put themselves first, others second and God last. Jesus wants you to put him first, others second and ourselves last. Being a Christian isn't about just knowing who Jesus is – it's about being friends with him and making him Lord of all our life. This relationship is different to the ones you have with your mates. There are challenges to being in a relationship with Jesus, but you can live your life with him, and he has promised to be with you wherever you are. This means that whatever you do, Jesus is there with you. (Check out Matthew 28:18-20).

You have friends because you take time to talk with them, and do stuff together. If you never talked to your mates then they wouldn't be your friends for long. If you want to know Jesus then you have to talk to him and spend time with him. Friendships don't just happen but they take time, effort and energy. We develop habits that help us become good friends like talking regularly, meeting up and having fun. In the same way we need to develop good habits to help us be better friends with Jesus. The great thing is that Jesus wants to have that friendship with you – he is just waiting for you to come and talk to him. Here are four helpful habits to practise:

1) MEETING UP WITH FRIENDS

Get together with some Christian mates. Meet with them once a week or whenever you can. Be honest with each other; talk about what makes it easy to be a Christian and what makes it difficult. Celebrate the stuff that's going well and support each other in the things that are tough. Good Christian friends will ask you the difficult questions and keep your relationship with God sharp. Make sure you also ask your friends those difficult questions too!

2) MEETING UP WITH CHURCH

God thinks church is great! Try and go whenever you can. Get involved in a Christian youth group where they don't just play pool and table-tennis but one where they study the Bible and worship God together. At church we spend time with other Christians and discover more about Jesus. Church helps us in our walk with God and should encourage us in the way we live out our faith at home, school, college and work.

3) TALKING TO GOD

Praying is simply talking with God. You can do it anywhere and at anytime. There isn't a magical formula to prayer. You don't have to shut your eyes and put your hands together, you just need to talk to God. Talk to him about whatever you want. It's good to tell God that we love him. It's good to thank him for what he does for us. Try telling God the things you are finding difficult and are struggling with. Try writing your prayers down, a list could help you remember what to pray for.

God speaks to us so we need to listen to him. God speaks to us through the Bible, and sometimes through other people. Sometimes we know that God is talking to us because we feel it deep down within us. Write down what you think he may be saying to you. If you're not sure if it's God speaking to you, why not talk about it with a Christian you trust?

4) ENJOYING THE BIBLE

Isn't it amazing that God wants to speak to us? One of the ways he will do this is through the Bible. In this amazing book we discover all about God and his plan for the world and our lives.

Get a version of the Bible that you understand. Have a look at www.biblegateway.com or ask a Christian you trust. The Bible is not there to sit on your bookshelf; God wants you to read it. The Bible is made up of loads of different books. Some parts of the Bible can be quite complicated to understand. It's probably worth getting some Bible reading notes to help you.

You could pick a book in the Bible and read through it, why not start with Luke, which is in the New Testament? You could also read it with a group of friends.

⚡ What can I do?

Being a Christian is not about being part of a secret society. God has changed your life, and that is news worth sharing. Tell your family and friends that you are a Christian, help them to understand why you believe in Jesus and want to put him first in your life. Pray for them that they may get to know Jesus too.

Being a Christian is about living for Jesus. You have got your whole life to discover more about him and his plans for you. Take your time and create habits that will last a lifetime. Think about getting involved in your local community; volunteer for a local Foodbank or other charity, or find out if you have skills that could help your church. Show the world God's love through your actions. Realise that you have been created by God, not by chance but by design and for a purpose. Enjoy the reality that God loves you.

Live life to the max!

➕ Where can I get more help?

- Go to page 66-71 for more information and recommended resources.
- Get involved in your local church.
- Get involved with your school or university CU.

Holy Spirit

There are some amazing high performance cars out there. With the best engines and mechanics, these cars are capable of pulling off immense speeds. It's funny to think though, without fuel in them, they're just metal boxes going nowhere.

It's the same with the Holy Spirit. Just as cars need fuel, we need the Holy Spirit to fill us.

Matthew 3:11 '"I baptise you with water for repentance. But after me comes one who is more powerful than I, whose sandals I am not worthy to carry. He will baptize you with the Holy Spirit and fire."'

WHO IS THE HOLY SPIRIT?

Jesus described the Holy Spirit as a 'person who helps another person.' The Holy Spirit helped the disciples all those years ago and helps us, today, as we follow Jesus.

When we choose to follow Jesus, the Bible says the Holy Spirit lives inside of us and gives us power to do amazing things. With his help we can make sense of stuff (John 14:26) and have power for all sorts of things including leadership (Judges 6:34), strength (Judges 15:14), and artistic work (Exodus 31:3).

This friendship, help and power to do things can be the normal experience for everyone who follows Jesus. Just like a lawyer defends someone by giving them wise instruction, comfort and good advice to help them through their case, God promises to give us the Holy Spirit to help us follow God.

There are loads of scriptures in the Bible about the Holy Spirit and God makes it clear that we need him to fuel us, in the same way that Jesus received power through the Holy Spirit. (Check out Luke 3:22).

The Bible says that God has given us the Holy Spirit to remind us of all the things he has taught us (John 14:26), so we always know that when the Holy Spirit gives us power to do something, it matches up with the teaching of Jesus. This way, we don't have to be driven by effort or emotion, but can do the amazing things God calls us to do, with the help of the Holy Spirit. It doesn't matter whether we're loud or quiet, outgoing or shy, he still works through us!

BEING FILLED WITH THE HOLY SPIRIT

Being filled with the Holy Spirit is often called being 'baptized in the Holy Spirit' and is different to being 'born again' and making a commitment to follow Jesus.

The Bible says that when we make a commitment to God, the Holy Spirit is given to us and we're called God's children and can live in close community with him (Romans 8:15). There are also distinct moments when people in the Bible were filled with the Holy Spirit to do incredible things such as share the good news about Jesus. (Check out Acts 1:8).

Jesus 'breathed' on his disciples saying, 'Receive the Holy Spirit' (John 20:22). Even though the disciples already believed and had seen loads of miracles, including Jesus himself raised from the dead, he promised them more! He said, "In a few days you will be baptised with the Holy Spirit" (Acts 1:5) and they were! Being filled with the Holy Spirit transformed a fearful bunch of men into courageous champions for God.

Have a read of Acts 2 in the Bible. It tells us what happened on the day when, as Jesus promised, the disciples were baptised with the Holy Spirit. This day we now call 'Pentecost.' In what was probably the most exciting house party in history, the disciples were overwhelmed with praise for God and did some amazing things. When the Holy Spirit filled them, it wasn't about a nice feeling or sensation, the disciples were given new languages to take the story of Jesus around the world.

THE GIFTS OF THE HOLY SPIRIT

The Holy Spirit living inside us not only gives us guidance and power but gifts – gifts for the Church that are needed for us to share God's good news.

Check out Romans 12 - it tells us that the Holy Spirit gives out all sorts of gifts to all sorts of people, all as an expression of God's power in action. God compares this variety of gifts to all the different bits of our bodies. Each bit has a role and function and no matter how many different body parts you can think of - limbs, organs, and cells - they're still all part of one body. And it's the same for us. The Holy Spirit gives different gifts to each of us, but all for one purpose, bringing us together so we're all on the same track with the same goal; to be his messengers, his voice and his body here on earth.

LOOKING AHEAD

With the Holy Spirit filling us and acting as our fuel, we're housing something pretty special! The Bible calls us "temples of the Holy Spirit" (1 Corinthians 6:19). When we're given very special and expensive gifts, we don't chuck them aside or put them in the bin. We know we've been given something of worth! It's the same with the Holy Spirit. We don't waste what God paid a high price for. His gift to us gives us power to do incredible things, as part of an incredible church and make God famous around the world.

So now we know the fuel we have inside us is no ordinary fuel and we can ask the Holy Spirit to keep filling us for the journey. Living with the Holy Spirit and following God is the greatest adventure we'll go on so buckle up and get ready for the ride of your life!

➕ Where can I get more help?

- Go to page 66-71 for more information and recommended resources.
- Talk to your youth leader or church leader about being baptised in the Holy Spirit
- Find people who can pray with you

Guidance

?! What's the issue?

We all have questions about what we are going to do with our lives, and most of us need some guidance! But when so many people offer advice, and the world is full of self-help books and chat-rooms how can we work out what God wants us to do? Does God speak to us and how do we do hear him?

The amazing thing is that God does want to speak to us! The Bible tells us that in the Old Testament God spoke through specific people at specific times - we call these guys prophets - people like Samuel, Elijah and Isaiah. However, in the New Testament, when Jesus came, something changed. God no longer only spoke through the prophets (Hebrews 1:1-2). God was now speaking to us through Jesus! And Jesus promised that the Holy Spirit would speak to and guide us all (John 14:26).

☹ Why me?

Here's a fact - God has a plan for your life – the Bible clearly says this (Ephesians 2:10). But how can we find out what this plan is? How does God speak to us? Well there are many ways, including:

- Through the Bible - this book equips us for life (See 2 Timothy 3:16-17 and Psalms 119:105) and God has already spoken to us through it. For example, we don't need to go to God to ask him whether we should lie because God has already told us in the Bible.
- Through his Spirit - if the Holy Spirit is living in us then God can continually speak to us and guide us. If we are doing something and are not comfortable doing it - ask the question - who is speaking and why?
- Through each other - God wants us to be part of his church because he uses us to encourage and speak to each other.

There are things that stop us hearing God's voice. Sometimes we hold on to stuff that we need to say sorry for, and this can stop us hearing from God (Isaiah 59:2). Sometimes we want an answer instantly when actually we need to be patient and wait (Lamentations 3:24-26, Psalms 27:14, Psalms 37:7, Psalms 40:1, Psalms 130:5). Sometimes we simply don't listen! John chapter 10 talks about us belonging to God and how we need to listen to him so that we recognise his voice and can be guided by him!

⚡ What can I do?

One of the best things you can do is put yourself in a place where you can recognise what God may be saying to you. If you know about any sin in your life, confess it to God and ask for his forgiveness, read the Bible, and listen to him. Sometimes we can complicate the issue when all we need to do is seek God with all our heart.

It is often confusing trying to work out what God is saying to you, but there are people and places that can help.

What does the Bible say?

Check out what the Bible says by reading the verses already mentioned, or those listed below:

Deuteronomy 30:19-20 'This day I call the heavens and the earth as witnesses against you that I have set before you life and death, blessings and curses. Now choose life, so that you and your children may live and that you may love the Lord your God, listen to his voice, and hold fast to him. For the Lord is your life, and he will give you many years in the land he swore to give to your fathers, Abraham, Isaac and Jacob'.

Proverbs 3:5-6 'Trust in the Lord with all your heart and lean not on your own understanding; in all your ways submit to him, and he will make your paths straight'.

Romans 12:1-2 'Therefore, I urge you, brothers and sisters, in view of God's mercy, to offer your bodies as a living sacrifice, holy and pleasing to God—this is your true and proper worship. Do not conform to the pattern of this world, but be transformed by the renewing of your mind. Then you will be able to test and approve what God's will is—his good, pleasing and perfect will.'

Where can I get more help?

- Go to page 66-71 for more information and recommended resources.
- Take time to pray and listen, and talk to your youth leader.
- Youth Bible (published by Word) lists loads of key subjects such as money, school, church, sex, etc, and tells you where you can find what the Bible has to say about them.

Forgiveness

?! What's the issue?

It's a sad fact that people do things that hurt us – sometimes by mistake and sometimes intentionally. We can be left feeling upset, angry and confused by their actions.

Sometimes we don't deal with these feelings very well – perhaps we're uncomfortable talking about them or don't know who to go to. Perhaps we don't want to excuse what has happened to us. So we hold onto the pain and anger. Maybe we want to get even with the person or people who hurt us.

The worst thing about this is that the person it really hurts is you. As you hold on to all the hurt, anger and bitterness, you're not free to move on and enjoy the awesome life God has in store for you. It's like a weight has been tied around you and you can't go forward. Forgiveness cuts you free from the weight of your past and let you move on into your future.

😞 Why me?

Well, it's difficult to answer that. We live in a world that is far from perfect where people can be selfish and hurtful. (I'm sure you can think of a time you've hurt someone – I know I can!)

It's important to say that forgiveness is NOT about forgetting or excusing what has happened to you. It does NOT mean that you shouldn't feel anger or sadness. It does NOT mean that God expects you to be best buddies with people who hurt you.

Rather, forgiveness is making a choice to let go of any resentment and blame you feel, to give God the responsibility for the person or people that have hurt you and to move freely into your future.

📖 What does the Bible say?

The Bible tells us that we should forgive any people who hurt us because it's the very best thing for our lives. It allows us to enjoy life free from past hurts and to experience a deeper relationship with God.

It also reminds us how God has forgiven each of us of all the things we have done to hurt him. When we forgive others, we're being just like God – and we have an amazing example in Jesus who freely forgave the people who crucified him (See Luke 23:34).

Don't just take my word for it, grab a Bible and check out these verses:

Luke 11:4 — 'Forgive us our sins, for we also forgive everyone who sins against us. And lead us not into temptation'.

Romans 12:17-18 — 'Do not repay anyone evil for evil. Be careful to do what is right in the eyes of everyone. If it is possible, as far as it depends on you, live at peace with everyone.'

Colossians 3:13 — 'Bear with each other and forgive one another if any of you has a grievance against someone. Forgive as the Lord forgave you.'

⚡ What can I do?

If you know you need to forgive someone, try following these simple 'ABC' steps…

Ask for help.

Talk to God and ask him to help you forgive. You could also find someone you trust to chat to and pray with. (Preferably someone older and wiser such as a youth leader or church leader).

Be honest.

Acknowledge the fact that you've been hurt (You could talk about it to God or another person). You might feel angry or sad – that's ok. Forgiving someone isn't easy!

Choose to forgive.

Remember – forgiveness isn't an emotion, it's a choice. (One you might have to make many times!) You might find it helpful to write a letter to the person who has hurt you saying that you forgive them. (You don't have to send it!) Or you could pray out loud with a person you trust, telling God that you want to forgive. If you feel able, you could tell the person face to face that you've forgiven them!

➕ Where can I get more help?

- Go to page 66-71 for more information and recommended resources.
- If this is an issue for you, please make sure you find a Christian adult or mature friend that you trust to chat to.
- If you want to be encouraged that forgiveness is possible then visit *theforgivenessproject.com* - It's full of amazing stories of people who have found the strength to forgive.

Occult

?! What's the issue?

There is a lot of confusion about what the word 'occult' means. The word is defined as 'hidden, secret, mysterious, supernatural influences'.

The occult may seem to be just a bit of harmless fun and parts of the media can portray it as that, but the reality is quite different. Nothing about the occult is good or harmless - although it may seem that way. If we get involved, we are opening ourselves up to dangerous supernatural influences and spiritual forces. The Bible makes it clear that the occult is against what God says is good for us.
(Check out Deuteronomy 18:9-11).

You may not even realise that some of the things you've been doing are part of the occult, or you may not understand that being involved in the occult puts you under Satan's influence. So what should Christians avoid? We suggest you should avoid astrology, fortune telling, horoscopes, hypnotism, levitation, Ouija boards, palm reading, psychic powers, séances, spiritualism, tarot cards, Wicca and witchcraft - black or white.

God's enemy, Satan, is behind the occult. The Bible warns us he is dangerous (1 Peter 5:8) and that he is the father of lies (John 8 :44). He wants to bring hurt, confusion, guilt and fear into our lives, and will do whatever he can to mess up our relationship with God.

😞 Why me?

The supernatural is what it says on the tin - beyond the natural order of things. It is exciting, fascinating and different to our every day experiences.

If you have ever been involved in any of the things mentioned above, or something similar, don't panic. Sometimes other people who are involved in the occult can affect us, so that we feel down and in the dark. It is said that white magic and white witches do good, but all supernatural power either comes from God or Satan, so if the person practising anything supernatural is not given power by being filled with God's Holy Spirit, the power is not from God.

Looking at the reality of the occult, if you or someone close to you, has played around with it, you may be affected by, in Star Wars speak, 'The dark side rather than the light.' But read on, help is at hand and God is LIGHT. (1 John 1:5)

💬 What does the Bible say?

The Bible warns us against all these things to do with the occult. (Check out Leviticus 19:31, Isaiah 8:19-20 and Deuteronomy 18:9-11).

Supernatural power comes from either God or Satan and Satan is very good at copying what God can do. (Look up Exodus chapters 7 and 8). The magicians of Egypt could copy what Moses and Aaron did by God's power, BUT their power from Satan was limited. Even the magicians had to admit defeat, with the power difference being "the finger of God". (Exodus 8:19).

God is more powerful than Satan.

2 Corinthians 10:3-5 'For though we live in the world, we do not wage war as the world does. The weapons we fight with are not the weapons of the world. On the contrary, they have divine power to demolish strongholds. We demolish arguments and every pretension that sets itself up against the knowledge of God, and we take captive every thought to make it obedient to Christ.'

Jesus died to defeat Satan's power over us.

He has the power to destroy occult, supernatural influences, set you free, and give you a clean start.

1 John 3:8 'The one who does what is sinful is of the devil, because the devil has been sinning from the beginning. The reason the Son of God appeared was to destroy the devil's work.'

Hebrews 2:14 'Since the children have flesh and blood, he too shared in their humanity so that by his death he might break the power of him who holds the power of death—that is, the devil.'

Jesus gave his supernatural power to his disciples.

Luke 9:1 'When Jesus had called the Twelve together, he gave them power and authority to drive out all demons and to cure diseases'.

God gives supernatural gifts by his Holy Spirit.

(Check out 1 Corinthians 12:1-11).

⚡ What can I do?

- If you have personal experience of the occult, you will need to ask Jesus into your life to get rid of anything that is damaging to you, and fill you with the power of the Holy Spirit - the ultimate and all-powerful positive influence. (See New Life on page 5 on how to do this).
- We can resist the devil and his tricks by putting on the armour of God (Ephesians 6:10-18).
- Don't look at stuff about the occult or fill your head with films, TV, games and magazines that focus on 'the dark side'. Instead 'whatever is true, whatever is noble, whatever is right, whatever is pure, whatever is lovely, whatever is admirable—if anything is excellent or praiseworthy—think about such things' Philippians 4:8.

➕ Where can I get more help?

- Go to page 66-71 for more information and recommended resources.
- Talk to your youth leader or church leader about your experiences and get them or another experienced Christian to pray with you about this.

Relationships

Domestic Abuse

Abuse in the family is abusive behaviour from a family member or partner. Abuse is used to make the other person fear the abuser and do what they want. It usually begins with little things but progressively gets much worse.

Domestic abuse is also called domestic violence or intimate partner violence (Women's Aid definition of Domestic Abuse). It happens when one person hurts or bullies another person physically, sexually, psychologically, emotionally, socially or financially within an intimate or family-type relationship. This includes forced marriage and so-called "honour crimes". It can happen between people who are dating, living together, have children together or are married to each other. It can happen either when people live together or separately. It can happen after the relationship or marriage has ended. It can happen to people who regularly attend church and are Christians.

In most cases (but not always) it is the man who is the abuser and the woman or child who gets hurt. Domestic abuse is a repeated pattern of behaviour and is used to control other people. There are many ways in which a person can abuse others and these behaviours may get worse the longer the two people are together. These may include:

- Constantly putting a person down or criticising them (e.g. telling them they are a bad mother or bad wife).
- Telling them they are ugly, too fat/thin, stupid, useless, etc.
- Treating them as a servant/slave.
- Constantly checking where someone is.
- Preventing them from seeing friends or family.
- Not letting them get a job or making them work long hours or 2 jobs.
- Shouting, smashing things, throwing things, sulking.
- Hitting, pushing, slapping, kicking, and pinching.
- Threatening to hurt someone they care about such as the children or their pets.
- Rape or making someone do sexual things they don't want to do.
- Using scripture to justify their behaviour e.g., 'I'm the head of the house and you submit to me.'
- Not giving them any money, taking all their money from them or checking what they spend money on.

If any of this is happening in your family, remember that you are not alone. Domestic abuse happens in all types of families and there are people that can help you and your family.

Everyone has the right to be and feel safe.

'There is no fear in love. But perfect love drives out fear, because fear has to do with punishment. The one who fears is not made perfect in love.' 1 John 4:18

😟 Why me?

Although domestic abuse happens mostly between adults, young people can be significantly damaged or manipulated as part of domestic abuse or be victims of abuse themselves. Many young lives are affected by the abuse in their homes. A child who witnesses domestic abuse is exposed to abuse. Domestic abuse can have serious long-term impact on children and young people. Young people and teenagers may also experience abuse in their relationships, from their own boy/girlfriend. "Sexting" and "revenge pornography" are ways in which a person can be humiliated by their partner.

You may be aware of/experiencing domestic abuse in your home. Remember, people who abuse others are making a choice to do so. If someone in your family is abusive, it's not your fault. You can find help even if you have been told to keep it 'secret'. No two families are the same. Yet, healthy and loving relationships are possible and God-intended. You deserve to be in a family that chooses to be a safe, nurturing, respectful and loving environment!

(For more information on children's and young people's rights go to page 68).

A healthy relationship is when two people treat each other as equals, they trust each other and treat each other with respect. In a healthy relationship, people should support and respect each other. Disagreements can be resolved through talking and listening to each other's views and feelings.

When a person chooses to abuse and cause fear in others, that is not love. Fear is not healthy. Inequality and a lack of respect cannot exist in a loving relationship.

📖 What does the Bible say?

God is love and gives us the freedom to have a loving relationship with him. We can choose to demonstrate our love for him and reflect his love for us by having loving, healthy relationships. God does not force us to love him. Just as God never humiliates or belittles us, a man who loves his partner must treat her with respect. Jesus always treated women with dignity and respect.

Domestic violence is in stark opposition to God's plan for families. Right from the book of Genesis, marriage is depicted as a helping relationship. In Ephesians 5:21-33, we see that men and women have to submit to each other. Marriage is seen as an image or reflection of Jesus' love for the Church. Husband and wife belong to one another and are called to love one another as Christ loved us. There is no room for domestic violence in this relationship.

Following Jesus involves serving others with love, not manipulating and controlling them. He commanded us to "love one another" (John 13:34). Family relationships are meant to reflect God's love. God grieves when a home turns into a place of fear, suffering and pain. God's desire for those involved with domestic violence - both victims and abusers - is healing and wholeness.

I have a question...

"I just want the abuse to stop – what can I do to make it stop?"

Answer: You need to understand that just as you are not responsible for the abuse, it's not your responsibility to stop the abuser from harming you or to protect your parent from abuse. The abuse definitely needs to stop, but no matter how strong you are, it's not your responsibility to stop.

The first thing you need to do is reach out for help and be safe. Please talk to someone you can trust, someone you feel comfortable talking to – this could be your youth worker, teacher or best friend's mother. It takes a lot of strength to talk about your situation. By seeking help you are being very brave. If you feel uncomfortable talking to people you know, you can contact one of the support agencies or helplines listed at the back of the book (See page 68 for more information)

"When my dad slaps my mum I want to protect her. Should I get involved?"

Answer: No, it is not your responsibility to stop the fighting and protect the parent who's being hurt. It can be very dangerous if you intervene and puts you at risk of getting hurt. It could also make things worse. If you're really worried about your parent being hurt, call the police on 999 for free and ask for help. You can do this from your home phone, mobile or from a friend's home if that is the safer option.

"I can't understand why mum doesn't just leave my dad. He's so mean to her."

Answer: This is a question that gets asked a lot. There are many reasons why someone might stay in an abusive relationship. If it was easy, of course a woman would leave the abusive partner. It's possible that...

- They don't know where else to go or get help.
- They may still love their partner.
- They may have stopped believing in themselves and feel like they can't cope alone.
- They hope their partner will change and the violence will stop.
- They don't want to take their children away from the other parent.
- They don't have the money to leave.
- They don't feel strong enough to leave.

Just like you might feel confused about what's happening, your parent might also feel confused about what to do. If you have questions about what's going on, don't be afraid to ask. Sometimes it might be difficult for your parent to talk to you about the violence because they want to protect you. Also, perhaps we should be thinking of what the abuser should or should not be doing. The victim is not responsible for the actions of the abuser. For the abuse to stop, the abuser needs to make a decision to stop, to change.

"Things are getting really bad at home, is there somewhere safe we can go?"

Answer: If you or your mum is being abused, you can move into a refuge. As well as refuges, most areas have a local support services that can discuss other options for you and your family. (See page 68 for more information)

"I want to run away, should I?"

Answer: If you're unhappy at home, it's natural that you might think about running away. But it isn't the answer. Running away can be dangerous because it can be difficult to find somewhere safe to stay. It's important to try and get help whilst you're still at home. If you feel like running away, try to call a helpline or talk to someone you trust. You could perhaps arrange to go to their place for a bit or somewhere else you know is safe.

"Does God really know what is happening in my home? Why would he allow it?"

Answer: God says in Isaiah 43:2 'When you pass through the waters, I will be with you; and when you pass through the rivers, they will not sweep over you. When you walk through the fire, you will not be burned;the flames will not set you ablaze.'

He knows what you are going through and has great compassion for you. For he says in Isaiah 49:15 'Can a mother forget the baby at her breast and have no compassion on the child she has borne? Though she may forget, I will not forget you! See, I have engraved you on the palms of my hands'.

Remember, there is no judgement from God, only love and compassion. It is understandable if you feel hurt and let down by everybody, including God. You might even feel ashamed for yourself and your family. As you begin to cry out to him in hurt, in anger, in confusion and desperation, he will hear you and restore you. Healing is a process and doesn't happen instantly. Don't feel rushed or pressured to forgive the abuser. True forgiveness brings freedom to the ones who are victims of abuse but cannot happen till the truth and seriousness of the situation are acknowledged and addressed. You will most likely need the help and support of a trained counsellor to help you walk through the healing process.

Psalms 55:16-17 'As for me, I call to God and the Lord saves me. Evening, morning and noon I cry out in distress, and he hears my voice.'

✚ Where can I get more help?

- Go to page 66-71 for more information and recommended resources.
- If this is an issue for you, please make sure you find a Christian adult or mature friend that you trust to chat to.

Written by Restored Relationships

Family

?! What's the issue?

No two families are the same. As well as being made up of people of different ages and with different personalities, family structures also vary. There are families comprising mother, father and children, single parents and children, grandparents and grandchildren, step-families, brothers and sisters with no parents and many more.

Families are the foundation of society and have the greatest potential for nurturing and raising healthy individuals. But when families break down they can also wound their members badly.

☹ Why me?

You may be reading this because you are struggling with your family situation. You may find it hard to get along with your parents and brothers and sisters – your dad may be insensitive, your mum infuriating, and your siblings annoying and frustrating. On the other hand, you may really enjoy being with your family, but are worried and stressed by the illness of a parent, sibling, or other family member.

Every family experiences good and bad times, so don't feel ashamed or guilty if you are struggling, or feel that no-one else will understand. And if a member of your family is hurting you, it is important that you tell an adult you trust – a youth worker or teacher, perhaps – or you can call one of the phone numbers at the end of this booklet.

⚡ What can I do?

God is more concerned about the quality of love that we have in our relationships than he is about how perfect our parents are, or how perfect we are. Members of our family may be letting us down, or we may not be behaving as we should towards them, but God's relationship with us as his children can deal with this. In grace, forgiveness, and unconditional love, God never stops believing in us. He never gives up on us, delights in us, and loves us anyway. We can pray that in all our family relationships, with God's help, we can show something of the same grace, forgiveness and unconditional love.

- Ask God to help you understand your family, and to show you how to cope with the situation you are in.
- Look at what the Bible says about families.
- Have a chat to someone like a youth leader and get them to pray with you.
- If a member of your family is hurting you, talk about it with someone you trust.

What does the Bible say?

Happy Families?

Did you know that many of the families in the Bible are by no means perfect? In fact they had all manner of issues. There is no such thing as a 'normal' family.

- Cain killed his brother Abel because he was jealous of him (Genesis 4).
- Joseph's older brothers not only attacked him, but they also faked his death and sold him into slavery (Genesis 37).
- Samson's wife tricked him and gave him to his enemies (Judges 16).
- The sons of King David betrayed him and nearly stole his kingdom (2 Samuel 15).
- Martha yelled at Mary when Jesus visited (Luke 10).
- Jesus' own brothers doubted him (John 7).

The Bible is full of many people from dysfunctional families, but God was still able to use them. However weird your family situation is, God can use you and bring good things out of every situation.

 ## I have a question...

"My parents are getting separated / divorced. I'm scared it's my fault, and also worried about what my life is going to be like now they're splitting up."

Answer: When your parents are going through a separation or divorce, remember that you are not to blame. Your parents' decision to split up may have been a difficult one, and hopefully you will be able to talk to them about their reasons for doing so. The marriage has failed, but they are still your parents and you are still their child. Your aim is to keep talking to both parents and, as far as it is within your power, to maintain a good relationship with them. Although life might feel uncertain or scary at the moment, remember that you are loved by God and that he will take care of you.

"I have a family member who is seriously ill. What can I do?"

Answer: One of the most difficult things to deal with is when a member of your family is seriously ill. You might feel worried, frustrated, scared or even angry at the situation. Or you may go through times when you are in shock and feel nothing at all.

In Mark 4:35-41 the disciples are scared – they are in danger of drowning. But they get Jesus involved and he commands the storm to die down. Jesus may not always remove suffering when there are hard times, but he promises to be with you when things are difficult. Remember that God said, "I will never leave you nor forsake you." (Joshua 1:5). God often uses us to help one another, so do talk to friends, a youth leader and other Christians.

If you are finding it difficult to pray, why not try writing a letter to God telling him how you feel, or get someone at your youth group to pray with you. Ask God to help you to support your family member, and let them know that you are there for them and will be praying for them.

"I can't stand my siblings! How am I supposed to cope?"

Answer: Although you might not get along with your brother or sister, it is helpful to try and understand where they are coming from. You never know, you might find one or two things that you have in common with them, or even find out that you can hang out with them!

Choose your battles carefully – small things are not worth falling out over right now – a good relationship with your siblings in the long term is so much better.

Try this activity:

Think about a difficult issue you need to discuss with your brothers or sisters, then take a piece of paper and draw a line down the middle. On one side write the heading 'How I feel about this issue', and on the other side write 'How [your sibling's name] feels about this issue'. Now try to fill in both sides of the paper. Don't talk to your brother or sister until you have made a real effort to fill in their side of the page.

"How do I get a good relationship with my parents?"

Answer: One of the most frequent things teenagers say about their parents (and vice-versa) is: "They never listen to me!" Often, too, it feels easier to talk to your friends rather than your parents. But having a good relationship with your parents is about communication and respect. Treat them as they you would like to be treated – one of the Ten Commandments is 'Honour your father and your mother.'

Make sure that you talk to them about things – your dreams, ambitions and fears, and – even though it may not be easy – the things that you are finding difficult. Why not ask your parents to go with you for a walk, or even out for a coffee, so you can have a one-to-one chat?

"My parents put way too much pressure on me. They are always forcing me into school work or things that I don't want to do. I just feel like I'm going to let them down."

Answer: Most parents want their children to achieve their potential and want to encourage them to work hard so that they get the most out of their education, but sometimes they may not be doing this in the most helpful ways. Try talking to your parents to make them aware of how pressured you feel, as they might not see that their expectations hurt you. Tell them about your dreams and ambitions and ask them to help you achieve these. Of course, your parents may not always approve of or share your dreams, and you may need to be ready to compromise. That may sound hard, but if you can show that you are willing to meet them half way, they may be willing to compromise with you.

➕ Where can I get more help?

When there are family problems, the best thing you can do is not bottle your feelings up. Why not talk to your church leader, your youth worker or someone else you can really trust. They will be able to pray with you and give you advice and helpful tips.

Go to page 66-71 for more information and recommended resources.

Questioning Your Sexuality

?! What's the issue?

Who we find attractive often plays a big part in how we see ourselves and in how we feel others can see us. At times it can feel like it defines who we are and what our future will be.

Homosexuality, Same-Sex Attraction, Gay, Lesbian or however you choose to label it - some of us find ourselves attracted to the same sex.

There are also some of us who find both the same and opposite gendered people attractive. This is often known as being bisexual.

Of course there are those of us who simply don't find anyone sexually attractive at all and this is often known as being asexual.

For many of us at different points in our life we can seek to question what label fits us best in the quest to know who we really are.

The truth is - we are way more than our sexuality!

We are ALL made by God.

We are ALL loved by God.

We are ALL created uniquely and each and every one of us is attracted to different types of people.

☹ Why me?

There are no formal statistics of how many people identify as being attracted to the same sex. There are two main reasons for this: firstly, sexuality isn't always easy to attach a label to, and secondly, it can often be difficult for people to share how they identify sexually. As Christians some of us can worry about sharing or owning our sexuality because we might worry about what others might think or how people might treat us if they know we experience same-sex attraction.

Fear can keep even the most confident person silent.

However, it is safe to say that there are many Christians who find people of the same sex attractive. So if you find people of the same sex attractive you are definitely not alone!

Our identity is so much bigger than whom we find attractive though. As Christians our primary identity is that of a child of God.

What does the Bible say?

The Bible contains only a few verses that discuss same-sex relationships, and there are many different theological views that stem from them.

Christians disagree about what the verses actually mean and how they should be applied to today's world. This can mean that the churches we find ourselves in might have a very different response to the topic compared to other churches.

These differences can make it hard for us to understand what the Bible wants to say to each of us today.

But remember that this is not a new thing. For centuries Christians far more intelligent than us have been trying to discern what the Bible does say about many difficult issues, and they haven't always been able to agree.

So whilst not all Christians or even all churches agree on a definitive 'This is what the Bible says' we can all agree that God is love.

We all agree that God knows each and every one of us. Jesus' life, death and resurrection truth is based on his identity and not on how we self-identify sexually.

The Truth

Whoever you find yourself attracted to or however you decide to label your sexuality, there are some amazing things about you that are 100% true.

God loves you and cares about all of you - including the bits that no one else knows about and even when you feel far from him. He loves you with an unconditional love that cannot be matched by any one else. Thankfully there is nothing you can do to change this. God's love for you is not dependent on who you find attractive or your sexuality. God knows you better than you know yourself. He knows your fears and your hurts. Don't take our word for it. Check out these verses in the Bible for yourself:

- God sees you as his child (John 1:12)
- God has known you since he knitted you together in your mother's womb (Psalm 139)
- You cannot be separated from the love of God (Romans 8:35-39)
- In Jesus there is no condemnation (Romans 8:1-2)
- You can come to God with total confidence (Hebrews 4:16)
- God has amazing things for you to do for him (Ephesians 2:10)

⚡ What can I do?

It can be lonely and difficult as a Christian to safely explore your sense of sexuality and identity. This often means that we can seek unhealthy ways and places to explore who we are in secret. Some of us can find ourselves living double or even treble lives and this can result in us feeling guilty, ashamed and isolated from both God and others

Speak Up

Ever heard an adult say something like 'Yeah we can have a chat but I can't promise to keep everything you say a secret'?

This can put a lot of people off talking to a youth worker or a church pastor about sexuality, but please understand that your sexual identity is not something that needs reporting. Your identity is personal and confidential to you.

Youth workers and pastors should only ever report stuff when there's a risk of danger to yourself or others – to do with safeguarding. That's the only time they would need to say anything to a professional like the Police or Social Services.

So - sharing with a responsible adult that you trust can be positive. Sharing that you have been finding people of the same sex attractive or that you are questioning your sexuality should not result in them telling anyone.

They will be able to listen to you, give advice and help you find local services that might be useful. They will also be able to pray with you, and ask God to continue to show you how much he loves you.

Seeking God

When you start to question your sexuality or find people of the same sex attractive you may only want to spend time studying what the verses in the Bible say on the subject. Others may find themselves withdrawing from acts of worship, prayer and Bible reading all together.

As we have said throughout, you are more than your sexuality and we would encourage you to find ways to keep seeking God.

It's important to be part of a church where you feel comfortable and accepted as a child of God. As we've mentioned, Christians hold different views on sexuality, so different churches handle this issue in different ways. Finding a church that holds similar values to you can be really helpful.

- Try following a set of daily devotion notes or undertake a Bible reading plan.
- Find people that you can pray with.

Remember God is interested in all aspects of your life and wants you to share your whole self with him not just this part.

➕ Where can I get more help?

- Go to page 66-71 for more information and recommended resources.
- If this is an issue for you, please make sure you find a Christian adult or mature friend that you trust to chat to.

Written by Ems Hancock

Sex

?! What's the issue?

Sex is everywhere, it's in nearly every film, TV programme, advert and magazine. Sex is used to sell us stuff, get our attention, and make us feel like we're missing out. That's a great shame because **God invented sex, and he made it good, he made it so that we could experience deep intimacy.**

The question is, what is the best context for sex? Sex is powerful, if we mistreat it we can get hurt and hurt others. It was designed to be a spiritual, physical and emotional bond with one other person. It's designed to be a force for good. That's why Christians talk about saving sex for marriage. It's not all about how long we have to wait, but how we create the type of relationship that deserves the commitment involved in marriage and sex.

We find there are a lot of myths when it comes to sex:

MYTH ONE: 'Everyone is doing it!'

At school you might hear people showing off about their exploits. You might feel left out if you don't join in or have any experience yourself. Did you know, most young people don't lose their virginity until they're over 16?

MYTH TWO: 'Sex is dirty'.

St Augustine did a lot of good, but he also told us that sex is disgusting and the church is still recovering. He was wrong on that one! Sex is good. The challenge for disciples of Jesus is to ask him to guide us as we express our desires in ways that are good for us.

MYTH THREE: 'Condoms = safe sex'.

The only perfectly safe sex is…no sex! As we saw earlier, sex is powerful. It can create a new life, it's powerful enough to join two people together (Matthew 19). If you know of someone who is having sex (whether you agree with what they're doing or not), you should get them to think about contraception, but that's not enough. Think about safety in these areas; spiritual, emotional, intellectual, recreational, and even financial. A healthy relationship needs to include all of these.

MYTH FOUR: 'If you've had sex, you can't be forgiven'.

This one is simple: There's no sin that is bigger than God's ability and willingness to forgive. See Romans 8:1. We often have a hard time accepting or understanding God's forgiveness, but that doesn't make it any less real.

BUT REMEMBER:

- People can struggle with guilt because of their sexual past, but there is nothing that God cannot forgive or restore.
- Don't have sex until you're ready. If you feel that sex or any sexual act is being forced on you, you have the right to say no. Then tell someone about it.

What does the Bible say?

Matthew 19:5 'Therefore a man shall leave his father and his mother and hold fast to his wife, and the two shall become one flesh.'

1 Thessalonians 4:3-4 'It is God's will that you should be sanctified: that you should avoid sexual immorality; that each of you should learn to control your own body in a way that is holy and honourable'.

Romans 8:1 'There is therefore now no condemnation for those who are in Christ Jesus.'

?! How far is too far?

We've probably all joked about this one, we've certainly all thought about it, and someone somewhere has probably given us 'the talk'. Are you satisfied with the answer to 'how far' you can physically go with a boyfriend or girlfriend without breaking any rules?

Why do we ask 'How far is too far?' Perhaps it's because we know or feel that desire and sex are good things. We're aware that Christians talk about saving sex until marriage but it's not always clear exactly what this means. It might be that we're already trying to bend the rules on this imaginary scale or find loopholes.

Let's talk about the scale...

It probably starts with hand-holding and ends with penetrative sex. The goal seems to be to get as close to sex as possible without actually 'doing it'.

It's not rocket science, everyone knows that sex can be good. Your desire for physical intimacy is a God-given thing, it's how you were made. When we start to be physically intimate, we kick off a very powerful set of chemical and emotional reactions, almost like our bodies were programmed for sex. As we've said, the Bible is really clear that sex is powerful.

That's why it should have boundaries. The Bible - God's Word - speaks of sex in lifelong, faithful, and monogamous relationships. We call it marriage. Marriage is designed to provide a safe context for the incredibly powerful and amazing gift of sex, with a lifetime to perfect it.

This is intimate stuff and it's worth pointing out that there are other great forms of intimacy which are just as important and powerful as the physical. We need to think about our spiritual, emotional, intellectual, recreational, and even financial intimacy. Let people into these areas carefully. If they're trustworthy they will be patient with you and enjoy the adventure of getting to know you. Demand deep levels of commitment for deep levels of intimacy, it's the safest way for you both.

Perhaps the question we should be asking one another is, 'How far is good for us?'

Ultimately, there is no definitive scale to work to. You have to decide where to draw these boundary lines for yourself. It's a part of growing in maturity. But you're not in this relationship thing alone, so here are some good suggestions for you and the person you're dating:

Talk about physical boundaries.

Don't do anything that you're not able to talk with each other and trusted friends/leaders about. Don't just let it happen, talk about it!

Chill out!

Enjoy the journey of building a healthy relationship not just the end result. Slower is generally better.

Build friendship.

Get to know each other, find out the things they like doing, what makes them laugh, appreciate good things about them, and talk about what you find difficult.

Get support.

All of our relationships need support and romantic ones are no different. Talk about your relationship with your parents and youth leaders, and don't be scared to ask for advice!

Just the two of us?

Your relationship will be better if you don't pretend you're the only two people left on the planet! Introduce them to your friends, meet theirs. You'll learn a lot! Your relationship could be a gift for others too.

WHAT IF YOU'VE ALREADY HAD SEX?

This stuff applies to all of us and remember that our past relationships don't have to define our future ones - we can learn and grow. We can build healthy relationships at any time.

⊕ Where can I get more help?

- Go to page 66-71 for more information and recommended resources.
- Check out what the Bible says
- Pray and talk to your youth leader or someone you can trust.

?! What about masturbation?

I think one of the reasons masturbation is difficult to talk about with others is that it generally happens when we're alone. Is it wrong for Christian guys and girls? The simple answer is that it depends.

The Bible doesn't talk about masturbation, certainly not in the way we'd think about it in the western world. (Did you know, some cultures don't even have a word for masturbation?) There isn't a verse that says 'No masturbating!'

Instead, when Jesus talked about sex, he was clear that it starts with our minds and hearts. He said '…I say to you that everyone who looks at a woman with lustful intent has already committed adultery with her* in his* heart.' Matthew 5: 27-34.

*Not just for boys!

What is Jesus saying? He's saying that our intentions matter and that if our intent is to consume the other person, to use them for our selfish pleasure, we're going against God's best for them and us. He's saying that the thoughts in our minds can go against what God wants for us and others. The Bible calls it 'sin'.

So masturbating to an image or video of someone or something you read where our intent or fantasy is to use this for our own pleasure; that's the kind of thing that's included in what Jesus is saying.

Some thoughts:

- Consider the kind of things you're spending time thinking about, are they fantasies that fit with God's plans for sex?
- It's ok for us to enjoy touch. You're developing as a sexual being, it's something God has placed within you for enjoyment! Think about what boundaries you think fit with what you find in the Bible.
- Remember you're not the only one dealing with this.
- Struggling with this stuff doesn't mean God loves you any less. He loves you!
- You may like to reflect on Philippians 4:8.

⊕ Where can I get more help?

- Go to page 66-71 for more information and recommended resources.
- Check out what the Bible says. (Youth Bible (Published by Word) lists loads of key subjects such as these and tells you where you can find what the Bible has to say about them.)
- Pray and talk to your youth leader or someone you can trust.

Written by Ems Hancock, Robin Rolls and Jason Royce

Watch What You Watch (Pornography)

?! What's the issue?

Incredibly, an apple or android smartphone has more computing power than Neil Armstrong's Apollo 11. Think about that next time you play Angry Birds! The internet - which hardly anyone even knew existed just twenty years ago - has made it possible to see almost anything, any time, anywhere.

That's a very good thing when it comes to researching your homework. But that same technology and those same powerful gadgets also put something much more harmful within easy reach - Pornography.

What is Porn?

Although that sounds like an obvious question, people have different ideas. So this is what the Collins Dictionary says "writings, pictures, films, etc designed to stimulate sexual excitement".

Thats means a book or a online story, a MTV video or even some stuff you do in some 18rated games like GTA, all can fit under that definition.

The average age that most people first see porn online is 11.

- 9 out 10 teenagers say they look at porn, often whilst doing their homework.
- The most popular porn website in the world gets 4.4 billion hits a month – only the likes of Facebook and Google get more.
- 12% of all websites and 35% of all internet downloads are pornographic.

And that's just the internet. With lads mags and newspapers, TVs in bedrooms or even mates texting pictures, it's never been easier for people to be exposed to porn every day.

Maybe that's how you feel? That porn is easy to find and so you just can't stop looking? Recent research among Christians suggests that we are just as tangled in the web of porn as anyone else.

😞 Why me?

Because you were made sexy! Sexual attraction is normal – in fact it's a good thing. We are made to desire beauty and be intoxicated by it (Check out Song of Songs in the Bible). You are a teenager, right now your body is changing and is releasing hormones that create desires and cravings that at times can SEEM uncontrollable.

BUT YOU CAN TAKE CONTROL.

Things people say about porn and what the Bible says

"It's harmless fun - a little bit doesn't hurt"

Looking at porn does feel good - although the shame and guilt never feels fun.

Some scientists even say the effect of seeing a pornographic image on a man is clinically equivalent to getting a hit off drugs. But like drugs, it's not harmless. Scientists who study the brain have discovered that porn quickly rewires our neural pathways (the way the brain works), affecting the way we think about relationships and the opposite sex and causes us to crave the very thing we are trying to stop doing. It other words, it can get addictive.

Porn is a liar. Promising fun but hiding the consequences. (Have a read of Proverbs 9: 16-18). God cares what you look at and what you fill your mind with. We should honour him with our body.
(See 1 Corinthians 6:18-20).

"I hate myself for not stopping"

We've all been there. You mess up and feel awful so decide "to never do it again" but then you mess up again. It's a pattern, the guilt and shame of failing yet again feels rubbish and it's difficult to imagine that changing. The only way to see change is with God's help. He wants to help. God loves you, forgives you, and wants you to know freedom. Confess your sins to God (Check out Psalms 51). He will forgive you; 'If we confess our sins, he is faithful and just and will forgive us our sins and purify us from all unrighteousness.' 1 John 1:9. God promises to help us to change. One main way he helps is through other people.

"I can't tell anyone about this"

Sin's power over us can grow when it's kept secret. It will take lots of courage but go to someone you trust (maybe your youth leader) and tell them about your struggle. Ask them for help in becoming who you really are. They can pray with you, ask you some tough questions every now and then, and help you get some things in place that will make a difference.

✛ Where can I get more help?

- Go to page 66-71 for more information and recommended resources.
- If this is an issue for you, please make sure you find a Christian adult or mature friend that you trust to chat to.

Written by Ian Henderson

Doing
Life

Addictions

?! What's the issue?

Addiction spoils us! We're unique, beautiful (yes you!), perfectly made (yes you still!), and God's favourite of all the things he created. Addiction to anything or anyone can spoil our families, ourselves, our relationships, our health, and even the communities in which we live. Addictions can be about sex and pornography, work, drugs, alcohol, self-harm, gambling and more. Let's face it; if you're reading this and you think you might have an addiction, you probably know it's not good for you. You might be aware of your behaviour changing, and the fact that you're trying to cover up your problem. Those are really natural things to do, and hundreds of thousands of people worldwide are addicts, so you're not alone.

☹ Why me?

There is often a reason why someone gets sucked into addiction. It could be any number of things and they will be different for each person. As you begin to deal with the addiction, it's just as important to deal with the root cause. If not, it will keep coming back to the surface and will continue to affect your life.

⚡ What can I do?

Well, you've taken a good first step, and if you have an addiction, then you've already done a brave thing by reading this. The first step on the road to a better tomorrow is to admit that things are not as they could be. Perhaps you might like to mention this to a trusted friend, or if you're a bit nervous about doing this then show them this book and issue and see if a conversation you're comfortable with starts that way. You might also like to try praying - somewhere quiet and alone, knowing that whoever you are, God is desperate to love you to bits and desperate for you to be whole again. It's important to find a bit more help because addictions are very hard to break on your own, and if your body has changed the way it normally functions because of an addiction, then it will be even harder to do without help from someone or something else.

📖 What does the Bible say?

The Bible doesn't talk a great deal about addictions, but we do know that Jesus wants to bring freedom where we are prisoners (Luke 4:18-19). Jesus' desire is to free us from all sorts of burdens and things that weigh us down (Matthew 11:28). In the Bible, there are different things mentioned about drink and sexual relationships, but we do know that God values our bodies as 'temples of the Holy Spirit' (1Corinthians 6:19). The overwhelming message throughout the Bible is that you are unique and precious to God, beautifully made, and he is proud of you, and excited by your very presence (Psalm 139). So being an addict is denying yourself some amazing opportunities to change and be free.

✚ Where can I get more help?

- Go to page 66-71 for more information and recommended resources.
- Lots of people can help you. Perhaps a youth worker or friend might be a good first step.

Written by Robin Rolls

Anger

Have you ever felt so angry you could explode? The truth is that we've all felt angry at some point in our life. Maybe it's the words people say or the things they do that make us furious. Or it might be the things we see happening around us. Whatever it is, we can react in a way that is angry! For some, this is an emotion they can't control and they end up hurting other people or even themselves. If that's you, if you'd say that anger is having a big say in how your life is going, read on.

Why me?

The world doesn't work the way God designed it to. When sin entered the world it was like a virus that affected everything. This means people don't treat others the way they should. We put "me" first and others second. We hurt and upset each other. This makes life difficult and can make us angry. But ultimately we choose how we react to situations. We choose how angry we get. We need to learn good habits so that we can control our anger… and not let anger control us.

What can I do?

1. Get Away

If you find yourself getting angry, get away from the situation! If there's a regular place you find you get angry, stop going to that place or walk away from the situation. If you can't easily leave, (like school), ask the teacher if you can leave for a few minutes. This will give you the chance to calm down and reassess the situation that is frustrating you.

2. Go To God

Talk to God about it. Be honest with him. He can handle you telling him how angry you feel; he's God after all!! Ask God to help you. It says in the Bible that, if we ask him to, the Holy Spirit can produce the opposite of anger in our lives - we become more peaceful, patient, kind and self-controlled.

3. Grab A Friend

A problem shared is a problem halved. Anger can make us feel under pressure. Talking about stuff we're angry about helps get rid of this pressure. Proverbs 17:17 tells us that a good friend sticks by us when we need them - find a friend who will help you. Find someone you trust and tell them you feel angry. Maybe you could find an older Christian that you trust and ask them if you can meet up regularly. Give them permission to ask you how you're doing with your anger. Ask them to tell you how they deal with situations when they get angry.

If you can't think of anyone to talk to, write down how you're feeling - this can also help get the anger out of your system.

What does the Bible say?

Ephesians 4:26-27   'In your anger do not sin: Do not let the sun go down while you are still angry, and do not give the devil a foothold.'

Galatians 5:16-25 shows us how to begin to live your life by the Spirit:

> So I say, walk by the Spirit, and you will not gratify the desires of the flesh. For the flesh desires what is contrary to the Spirit and the Spirit what is contrary to the flesh. They are in conflict with each other, so that you are not to do whatever you want. But if you are led by the Spirit, you are not under the law.

> The acts of the flesh are obvious: sexual immorality, impurity and debauchery; idolatry and witchcraft; hatred, discord, jealousy, fits of rage, selfish ambition, dissensions, factions and envy; drunkenness, orgies, and the like. I warn you, as I did before, that those who live like this will not inherit the kingdom of God.

> But the fruit of the Spirit is love, joy, peace, forbearance, kindness, goodness, faithfulness, gentleness and self-control. Against such things there is no law. Those who belong to Christ Jesus have crucified the flesh with its passions and desires. Since we live by the Spirit, let us keep in step with the Spirit.

✚ Where can I get more help?

- Don't bottle things up and try to handle things on your own.
- It often helps to chat through issues like this, so why not arrange to meet with your church leader, youth worker or someone that you really trust. They will hopefully be able to understand your situation, pray with you and give you some helpful tips.

Written by Mark and Liz Massey

Bereavement

?! What's the issue?

You're probably reading this because somebody close to you has died. Whether it was recently, or ages ago, we are really sorry, and wish you didn't need to read this.

When someone close to us dies, loads of feelings flood our minds. Sometimes we'll be sad. We might get angry, or frustrated. We might want to hit them because we blame them, or hug them because we miss them. We might have regrets or flashbacks. Sometimes we might think we just heard their voice. At other times we don't think about them at all. All these feelings are OK. They are normal! So don't worry if you've had them.

😣 Why me?

Death is one of the few things we all experience, nobody can avoid it, yet it is something we hardly talk about, and don't really know how to deal with. Ever wanted to punch someone who says they know how you're feeling?!

Unfortunately we can't change what's happened, but we can make sure we remember the person well, and in a way we feel comfortable with. And we can get some real help from Jesus, who is the one person who really does know how we feel.

⚡ What can I do?

It's good to remember the person in a way that's special to you. Maybe make a photo album of them, or collect some of their things together into a memory box? You could cook their favourite meal, or visit a place you remember going to together. Perhaps you just want to light a candle and listen to music while looking at a picture of them? Find something you feel is special to you and remember the person in that way. It's OK to cry. It's OK to smile when you think about them too!

💬 What does the Bible say?

Death sucks. It wasn't part of God's original creation. Genesis 3 lists the consequences of sin entering the world. Death is the climax of this list (v19). It's the worst thing possible on earth.

But flick to the end of the Bible. Heaven is described there, in another list. The writer can't wait to tell you something... there will be no more death! No more crying, no more pain (Revelation 21:4). Wow!

There's one more list, which helps us in the meantime. (Check out Matthew 5:1-12) Jesus has a huge crowd of people listening to him. The first people he speaks to are not the press, or the celebs, instead he says to those of us who mourn, who miss someone - there is comfort available! Jesus is able to comfort us in a way nobody else can. Spend time asking him to do this for you.

➕ Where can I get more help?

- Go to page 66-71 for more information and recommended resources.

Written by Paul Oxley

Bullying

?! What's the issue?

Being bullied is a horrible and damaging experience.

Nearly everyone has been bullied at some time in their lives. If you are being bullied, you may feel scared, lonely and vulnerable. If you are a bully, you may feel that you have got yourself into a pattern of behaviour that you can't get out of.

Either way, you owe it to yourself and others to try and sort out the situation so that the bullying stops. For many people, bullying causes huge stress and anxiety and can affect every part of their lives. The important thing to realise is that you can have control over what is happening. Remember that no-one deserves to be a victim of bullying.

☹ Why me?

You may have heard people say 'stand up for yourself'. That's all very well, but often the braver thing to do is to tell someone you trust. Even if you feel strong enough to deal with what is happening, there may be another person being bullied by the same person who is not. Telling someone about bullying isn't 'grassing' or telling tales. You and others have the right to be safe from attacks and harassment. Nobody can help you unless they know what is happening to you.

⚡ What can I do?

1. Tell an adult you trust

Bullying can be hard to talk about but you shouldn't feel that you have to handle it alone. Talk to an adult you trust. This could be your mum or dad, your aunt or a teacher. They will support you and help you to make it stop.

2. Talk to someone your age

Talk to a friend, or if you don't want to talk to someone you know, you can post messages and get advice on websites like Childline and Beatbullying.

3. Block the bullies

If you're experiencing bullying online, most websites will let you block people to stop them communicating with you. If you don't know how, there's lots of websites that can help you. Block instant messages and emails. Again, ask for help or look at the Chatdanger website for advice on how to do this.

4. Keep the evidence

Keep any tasty emails, texts or web pages so you can show someone what's been going on.

Report mean videos, pictures, comments or pages to the website you've found them on. If you need to, ask a parent or teacher for help with this, or look at Chatdanger, a website which has safety advice about mobiles and internet use.

5. Report serious bullying such as physical or sexual threats, to the police.

6. Don't retaliate or respond.

This is what the bully wants, and it might make things worse.

7. Don't struggle with this issue alone and don't accept bullying as acceptable behaviour

 ## What does the Bible say?

Remember that you are valuable and precious. Even if you hate the way you are acting at the moment, or the things that are happening to you, God can help you to overcome it. The Bible says in Isaiah 40:29 that that God 'gives strength to the weary and increases the power of the weak.'

Deuteronomy 31:6 'Be strong and courageous. Do not be afraid or terrified because of them, for the Lord your God goes with you; he will never leave you nor forsake you.'

Matthew 7:12 'So in everything, do to others what you would have them do to you, for this sums up the Law and the Prophets.'

1 Corinthians 16:14 'Do everything in love.'

⊕ Where can I get more help?

- Go to page 66-71 for more information and recommended resources.
- Check out what the Bible says.
- Pray and talk to your youth leader, and get someone to pray with you.

Depression

?! What's the issue?

We often use the term "I am depressed" when we are feeling miserable, sad or hopeless. Usually feeling this way passes when things look up a bit or we can change things. BUT if the feelings don't go away, or come back time and again and are interfering with your life, it could be an indication that you are suffering with depression.

This may be mild depression, which allows you to function pretty well, but everything is such hard work and your mood is low most of the time. Or it may be more severe, when you may struggle to function, you may stay in bed a lot of the time and you might want to give up. Whether mild or severe, this could be clinical depression, which needs help from a doctor.

☹ Why me?

You may feel depressed and desperate at points in your life, or you may feel helpless in changing your situation. This can happen for many different reasons:

- When family situations change.
- When a relationship breaks up.
- When someone close to you is ill or dies.
- You feel worthless and no good.
- When being abused, ill treated or bullied.
- You feel alone, unheard and not understood.
- You think that things will never improve and you feel hopeless and desperate in that.

It can also happen for no reason at all and as a result of brain chemistry going a bit awry.

How you cope with depression, desperation and hopelessness will either keep you going, or cause you to give up trying to change things and think of ending your life.

⚡ What can I do?

Recognise the signs; some of these may be:

- Sleeping too little or too much.
- Changes in eating patterns.
- Thinking negatively, always seeing things as awful.
- Being moody or irritable.
- Wanting to hide away.
- Crying a lot and easily.
- Feeling like harming yourself.
- Finding it hard to concentrate.

WHAT CAN I DO IF I THINK I'M DEPRESSED?

- Look after yourself physically. Try to eat and drink well, but alcohol doesn't help as it is a depressant.
- Take some exercise, even just walking round the block is a start, or going out to buy Haribo. Or play sport, jog, dance, anything that will make you active.
- Do things that make you laugh and be with people who make you laugh.
- Do things that you enjoy.
- Pay attention to how you look and sometimes treat yourself to something good.
- Challenge some of your negative thoughts, especially about yourself.
- Celebrate every little achievement (Taking a shower: managing to stay in school/ lesson).

GOOD friends can help you with all the above. They are very valuable and are great support.

Find someone to listen to your situation and how you feel. A counsellor at school, college or with a youth organisation may be available, or your GP could refer you. Try Youth Access for free counselling. Make sure you get on with your counsellor, OR change to one you do find helpful, this is essential.

If you are really low, cannot function and possibly have suicidal thoughts, you may need medical help before anything can be faced. This is not a weakness but a necessity, so a visit to your GP is the best start. Medication could be prescribed, again this can be very helpful and then counselling can become effective.

Many people think about ending their own life if they feel that their situation is hopeless, or they don't deserve help. But many find they CAN get help from others and can help themselves. You DO deserve help, whatever has happened to you and however you are feeling.

SO get help from others to move away from the desperation and the hopelessness you feel, by taking one step at a time to change your way of thinking and being.

What does the Bible say?

People in the Bible who had close relationships with God also felt depressed and hopeless. Look at King David and how he felt when his enemies were trying to kill him. Read Psalm 42 where David says he is mourning, in tears and downcast. He feels forgotten by God, but still tells himself to be positive and put his hope God.

Psalm139 v13-14 tells us that God knew what he was doing when we were first conceived and he wonderfully made us.

Zephaniah 3:17, tells us how God feels about us/you, however you feel about yourself right now:

'The Lord your God is with you, the Mighty Warrior who saves. He will take great delight in you; in his love he will no longer rebuke you, but will rejoice over you with singing.'

That delight, love and singing is not dependant on us, how we are, or what we do. It is unconditional, he made us, knows us and loves us and rejoices over YOU.

Jesus knew how tough life was and gave his disciples some encouragement in John 16:33 'I have told you these things, so that in me you may have peace. In this world you will have trouble. But take heart! I have overcome the world'. These words are also true for us

Remember God knows what you need, read Romans 8:26-28. In the same way, the Spirit helps us, using our weakness. We may not know what we ought to pray for, but the Spirit himself intercedes for us through wordless groans.

So stay with it, you can climb out of the pit of depression and hopelessness and move on with God.

👥 If your friend is depressed

Read all the above then:

- Be a person who really listens to them without judging or saying where they are wrong.
- Don't tell them to get over it.
- Don't tell them it is all a spiritual problem.
- Help them face one day at a time.
- Pray for them, (they may not appreciate you praying with them at first).
- Get professional help, start with their GP. Some schools and most colleges have trained counsellors who work with young people. Encourage them to make a self-referral. If this is not available, look up the Youth Access Website to check for local free youth counselling in your area.

If you are helping a friend who is depressed, get practical and prayer support for yourself.

➕ Where can I get more help?

- Go to page 66-71 for more information and recommended resources.

Written by Pauline Horder

Eating Disorders

?! What's the issue?

Most people think that eating disorders are just about food and weight. In fact they are much more complicated than that.

Often only you will know if you have an unhealthy relationship with food. If you think you may be developing some bad habits such as overeating, exercising excessively after eating, starving yourself, abusing laxatives, trying to be sick after food or anything else that you think may be an issue, then you'll need to get some help.

Recovery isn't just a matter of healthy eating and determination, but about understanding who you are in God, as well as how your emotions are tied up in your eating.

😔 Why me?

We may not always know exactly what has caused us to have an issue with eating. For some it is the result of some kind of life change or stress, such as a difficult family environment, the pressure of exams or friendships going wrong.

Whatever the root cause, eating issues are normally due to how we think and feel about ourselves. Whatever the cause of your personal issues, there is a God who loves you and understands what you are going through. There is some excellent help available. Well-presented websites and resources can help you to understand yourself better and what may be happening to your body.

⚡ What can I do?

1. Remember that it is possible to recover fully!
2. Tell a Christian friend or youth leader so they can pray with you.
3. See your GP for the best advice. You could also contact a charity.
4. Remember you aren't on your own. Thousands of people recover from eating issues of many kinds.

📖 What does the Bible say?

God thinks that you are amazing and whether or not you believe that – here is what the Bible says:

Psalms 139:13-14 'For you created my inmost being; you knit me together in my mother's womb. I praise you because I am fearfully and wonderfully made; your works are wonderful, I know that full well.'

Romans 8:16 'The Spirit himself testifies with our spirit that we are God's children'

Romans 5:8 'But God demonstrates his own love for us in this: While we were still sinners, Christ died for us'.

Go to page 66-71 for more information and recommended resources

Living An Ethical Life

?! What's the issue?

Take a look at your clothes. Where were they made and who made them? How were the people treated when they harvested or grew the products we buy in supermarkets or canteens? Did making these products harm the environment? Does the way we live everyday impact the environment?

As Christians are we up for challenging ourselves to reflect God's priorities whilst living in a consumer society? Should we also challenge the unjust and unethical structures that keep our global neighbours trapped in poverty and harm the environment?

It's a real struggle but are you ready to accept the challenge?

☹ Why me?

We believe it's easy to link our everyday decisions to others all over the world. If that's true then our actions have consequences that are much greater and far-reaching than perhaps we've ever thought before.

Martin Luther King Jr said, "Eating breakfast this morning, you depended on more than half the world." If we depend on so many people even before breakfast, we have a responsibility to ensure that they are treated fairly when they work for our benefit. And we have a responsibility as Christians to look after this amazing world that God has made.

But the exciting thing is you can make a difference!

⚡ What can I do?

- Firstly, start thinking about where and how you spend your money.
- Do you really need the things you buy, or are you buying them because you want the newest thing or the latest fashion?
- Is there an alternative with the Fairtrade mark on it?
- Shop loudly – write to the shops you spend your money in and ask them what their ethical policies are and how they look after their employees.
- Think about your own life – do you recycle your rubbish? Do you really need to make that car journey, or could you walk?

What does the Bible say?

Luke 10 tells the story of the Good Samaritan, and Jesus is asked who our neighbour is. His answer redefines who our neighbour is, it's not just the person in the house next-door, nor is it the person who crosses our path; it's anyone who needs us to step into their circumstances and help them.

Proverbs 13:23   'An unploughed field produces food for the poor, but injustice sweeps it away'.

✚ Where can I get more help?

- Go to page 66-71 for more information and recommended resources.

Loneliness

?! What's the issue?

Loneliness is a powerful feeling, which is not dependant on being physically alone - in fact we can often feel more alone when surrounded by a lot of people who we don't feel comfortable with. This is especially so when we are Christians and those around us are not.

Loneliness often affects us at points of change in our lives like going to a new school or when faced with a difficult problem. Sometimes there's a shift within friendship groups, where someone who was once your closest friend becomes friendlier with someone else. You may even feel as though you are not good at making or keeping the friends you do have.

☹ Why me?

Loneliness is a difficult thing to deal with but it is an issue that God understands. One of the lies of the Devil is that we are not special or important and this is the reason we are alone.

But God has never yet made a person who has nothing to offer the world. However you feel and whatever you have been told about yourself, there are things that only you can offer others.

⚡ What can I do?

Remember that even those who are always surrounded by friends feel insecure and lonely at times. Just because you are on your own does not mean that there is anything wrong with you. Remind yourself of friends you have made in the past and give yourself some time.

Try to be the sort of person that you would like to make friends with.

Talk and pray about it with a friend or youth leader.

📖 What does the Bible say?

God sees our heart and knows exactly how we are feeling.

In 2 Corinthians 1:4 he is described as the Father of compassion and the God of all comfort. Accept his comfort at this time. His love for you is abounding.

Isaiah 41:10 'So do not fear, for I am with you; do not be dismayed, for I am your God. I will strengthen you and help you; I will uphold you with my righteous right hand.'

Deuteronomy 31:8 'The Lord himself goes before you and will be with you; he will never leave you nor forsake you. Do not be afraid; do not be discouraged.'

➕ Where can I get more help?

- Go to page 66-71 for more information and recommended resources.

Written by Ems Hancock

More Than Bodies

(Sexualisation Of Girls)

?! Impossibly Beautiful - What's the issue?

Ladies, there are some amazing lads out there.

Mick and Jake are two such boys. I (Rachel) had been coaching them as peer leaders to help me deliver a sex and relationships programme in a girl's school, and they were brilliant at it. But one day as we were driving home from a session the guys spotted a gorgeous girl walking along the road and began to make a graphic list of all the things that made her 'fit'. I pulled over the car, ran up to this 'fit chick' and asked her if she would come and tell the lads a bit about herself - her name was Lucy, she was training to be a lawyer and she was married with a daughter called Chloe.

As we drove away Mick blurted out, 'Rachel, why did you do that? It was so awkward!' 'Boys, I'm not punishing you,' I replied. 'Lucy is stunning. But you disrespected her, her husband and daughter, when you treated her as if all she had to offer was how sexy she looked.' We're all guilty of doing it. But it's not OK when lads do it to us, and it's not OK when we do it to ourselves and each other.

WHY?

Because there is so much to you.

Think about it. You have a mind with thoughts crashing around it 24/7. You have emotions that flood your heart countless times a day. You have dreams, fears, passions, hobbies, disasters; you are one unique and beautiful woman. You're no accident or copy.

😔 Why me?

Have you ever heard of the word, 'Sexualisation?' It's the outcome of being treated as if there's nothing to you except your boobs, bum and face. Your sex appeal basically. It's a big lie that causes so much damage to so many girls and women. 9 out of 10 girls in the UK say they're unhappy with their bodies. (http://www.dailymail.co.uk/news/article-205285/90-teens-unhappy-body-shape.html#axzz2K7KkaElh). Why is this the case? Who are we listening to or comparing ourselves to? Could it be something to do with the culture around us?

MYTH ONE:
'YOU'RE JUST A BODY, SO FLAUNT IT!'

One of the big myths is that girls should be girlie and sexy. Who says? It sucks that society (and when we say 'society' we basically mean stuff like magazines, music videos, films, online world etc) wants to lock us into the idea that all we have to offer is our bodies. Even women we admire sometimes fall for it. But check out T4 presenter Jameela Jamil. 'I'm happy wandering around in my high-street clothes wearing no make-up. I'll be bringing my brain to the studio and that's all that matters.'

FACT 1
YOU'RE NOT JUST FOR SHOW –
YOU'RE TOO PRECIOUS FOR THAT.

MYTH TWO:
'YOU'VE GOT TO GET FIT TO FIT IN'.

Women's bodies have been intriguing men for years. Ever been in a museum and seen those nude paintings on pots from eons ago? Our bodies are gorgeous because God made them that way. Which means that we all have our own unique standard of beauty that is actually God's standard because he made us. We can't, and shouldn't, compare ourselves to how others look, but that's exactly what happens.

Take magazines. We're conditioned to see every girl in it as THE standard of beauty. But do you know what? In real life, without airbrushing and a whole make-over team, even the hot girl on the cover doesn't measure up to her own photo. Stupid eh? But it gets us every time.

FACT 2
YOU ARE YOUR OWN STANDARD OF BEAUTY.
COMPARING YOURSELF TO OTHERS WILL
ONLY MAKE YOU MISERABLE.

MYTH THREE:
'BE A BIMBO, BE BEAUTIFUL'

Have you noticed how photos don't talk? They don't age either. Or say the wrong thing, or have to shave their legs! Real life women (like you and us) do all these things – and more! We sweat, cry, have wonky teeth and bad wind after eating beans. But none of this makes us un-lovely or un-lovable. A society that likes girls to look like super models can't handle it when we act like the real people that we are, but we're not bimbos, or Barbie Dolls.

FACT 3
ONLY YOU CAN BE YOU.
DON'T WASTE TIME WISHING YOU WERE
SOMEONE ELSE.

What can I do?

So how do we respond to all this? What do you want to say to the culture around girls and women that can make us feel miserable and stressed about how we look and how we should act? Here's what Andrea came up with…

Dear Cultcha,

I'm writing because I need to tell you a few things. I know strictly speaking we're in communication all the time, but I don't think you're quite hearing me. I hate to tell you this so formally, but your services are no longer required. I serve a new God now and he's beginning to help me discover who I really am.

I know that to you my life might not seem perfect. At times it does feel like I'm struggling and I do feel rubbish about myself a lot of the time, but I don't think your suggestion of altering the way I look is very caring. In fact, I'm beginning to wonder if you ever cared. You almost had me convinced that I needed to lose weight – thank you for those 'celebs on the beach' pictures btw – but I've realised that no amount of dieting or exercising will cut it and that's okay! I'm determined to love my body because it's exactly that, mine. It's the only one I have so I need to look after it.

Your 'Essential Experience for Every Girl' packages are still selling really well, I see. In particular the 'Promise of Fame' package. When are you going to fess up and tell everyone that it doesn't come with actual self-esteem, just the illusion of it? It's called false advertising.

I hate to be the one to tell you this, but no matter how hard you try, I'll never lose enough weight, have enough clothes, fame, sexual partners or earn enough money to fill the space you've created.

I'm looking to God to find my identity. Unlike you, he genuinely cares about me and has made me impossibly beautiful. He's taking me outside of myself and allowing me to lift my eyes from the lies you keep spreading, to see the truth. You tell me it's impossible for me to ever be happy with myself (unless I spend LOADS of money on my appearance). But my uniqueness is what sets me apart so I'm looking no further than him from now on. Your services are no longer required.

So you do you, and I'll do me, okay?

Yours truly,

Womankind.

What would you say?

What does the Bible say?

- You are a unique and phenomenal woman, right from conception. (Psalm 139:15).
- God isn't impressed by beauty that is only skin deep. He's bowled over by your Jesus-like character. (1 Peter 3:3-4).
- Don't crave sex appeal, go after radiance! (Luke 11:36).
- When you said yes to following Jesus, influence and destiny was written all over you. (Mark 16:15).
- Use your body to honour God. Using it to chase guy-attention could create a neediness in you that will hold you back. (1 Corinthians 6:20).
- Fix your attention on who God says you are. He can renew your mind and help you see yourself as he sees you (Romans 12:1-2).

KAPOW!

'Av some of that!! Ladies, we are created with inner beauty, prized by God, and that pours out in our actions, expressions and courage, NOT the size of our waist or the length of our hair. If our focus is on these things then we are only headed to one destination – Dissatisfaction-ville. This is not a place we want to dwell in for any amount of time. Dissatisfaction often leads to many other unsavoury destinations, including, Anxiety Town, Self-Harm City and Eating Disorders HQ. Places that rob us of our God-given potential and vitality.

Here is a list of things to think about when striving to avoid a wrong-turn, even when our culture-satnav is telling us otherwise:

What makes you appealing to others is your beauty, and your beauty is shown in how you live your life:

- The way you care for others.
- The joy that lights up your face.
- The way you think through your options and make wise decisions.
- The love that you show your friends and family.
- The times that you take a stand against injustice.
- The difference you make in your school, community and home.
- The way you work hard to achieve your dreams.
- And the times you surrender your dreams for the sake of others.

A sexualised culture can make us afraid to let go and be true to who we are. But this is your one, wild life. You are free, in Jesus name, to live it to the full. Invite God to help you do that and kick 'sexualisation' in the face.

Written by Romance Academy

Self Harm

?! What's the issue?

You may be going through something really tough at the moment. It may even be hard to read these words because you are aching inside. You may feel so lonely that you are driven to anger and frustration - or beyond it. But hope and help are not as far away as they may seem.

There are all sorts of negative things that people do when they get stressed or worried. Maybe you are angry or anxious, so you hit out at something or someone, or it could be that you are incredibly tense and want a way out. You might feel alone, or neglected, as if no-one is really there for you.

One thing some people do when they feel like this is to harm themselves in some way. The problem with this is that it can leave them feeling worse. You may be hurting yourself. And you might not even know why you are doing it.

☹ Why me?

The problem is that our bodies can lie to us. If we hurt ourselves, the body tries to mask the pain by releasing something called endorphins. We know that these chemicals are addictive and can make people want to harm themselves again - to feel the same feeling. The result of this is that hurting yourself can become physically and mentally addictive.

These endorphins confuse the body into thinking that it is still functioning normally, even when it isn't. And so hurting yourself is dangerous and damaging.

Only you and God know how you feel right now. Even if you see no way out, there is one. You don't have to hurt yourself any longer. You may be surprised to know that there are some alternatives out there! Remember that God delights in who you are. He loves you passionately with a love that cannot be measured or changed or spoilt. He thinks you are amazing. He understands that you don't love yourself the way he does, but he wants you to learn.

📖 What does the Bible say?

Psalm 139 in the Old Testament is an amazing piece of writing which may help you to begin to understand how God sees you and how important you are to him.

⚡ What can I do?

There are ways you can help yourself, talking to a friend, doing some exercise or getting creative, can all enable us to express our feelings in safer and more constructive ways.

✚ Where can I get more help?

Check out what the Bible says, pray, talk to your youth leader and get someone to pray with you. It might also be a good idea to chat to your doctor to see if there is anything physical making you feel worse.

- Go to page 66-71 for more information and recommended resources.

Written by Ems Hancock

59

Self Image

?! What's the issue?

We all suffer from a lower self-image than God intended us to have. Even people who the world thinks are beautiful can be paranoid about part of their body, or how intelligent they appear. A famous supermodel, Cindy Crawford, is quoted as saying, 'Even I don't wake up looking like Cindy Crawford.'

Do you struggle with what you look like? Do you feel different to other people?

Do you feel anxious about your appearance or your speech, or the way you walk? Are you nervous that people won't like you?

Everyone has bad days, but if you tell yourself that you are no good at anything and no use to anyone, then you are wrong. Don't label yourself, and don't believe your own bad publicity.

☹ Why me?

We live in a world which is obsessed with outward appearance - any magazine you open has glamorous and 'perfect' bodies on the front. But the reality is that in God's sight YOU are just the way he created you to be. God did not make a mistake when he made you.

If you think that you are worthless, or you are unhappy with how you look, then this can affect you deeply and can have an impact on how you make relationships. Maybe the soundtrack of your mind replays phrases like "I wish I was pretty as her, or as funny, or as clever, or as popular…" Think about who may be telling you that. It is certainly not the voice of God. He calls you 'precious and honoured in his sight' (Isaiah 43:4) He doesn't say to you "Why can't you look like that?'

The reasons people feel bad about themselves are very different, but they have one thing in common - they can stop people reaching their full potential in God. Think about it, if you are always thinking negatively about what you look like, or what you can't do, you are not able to think about others. You simply haven't got enough room in your head.

It's important that you begin to talk to someone about how you feel. You may feel so disappointed with who you are that you are starting to hurt yourself in some way. Whatever the reason behind your feelings, it will help to share it with a Christian person you trust.

⚡ What can I do?

Check out what the Bible says and aim to believe it! (It may help to put some verses on your mirror or somewhere you can see them every day).

Pray, talk to your youth leader or a close friend, and get someone to pray with you.

Keep a journal so that you can write down any changes in how you feel.

What does the Bible say?

Genesis 1:26 explains that we are made in the very image of God.

Psalms 139:14-16 tells us that God is aware of every detail of our lives before we are even born.

Matthew 6:25-32 'Therefore I tell you, do not worry about your life, what you will eat or drink; or about your body, what you will wear. Is not life more than food, and the body more than clothes? Look at the birds of the air; they do not sow or reap or store away in barns, and yet your heavenly Father feeds them. Are you not much more valuable than they? Can any one of you by worrying add a single hour to your life? And why do you worry about clothes? See how the flowers of the field grow. They do not labour or spin. Yet I tell you that not even Solomon in all his splendour was dressed like one of these. If that is how God clothes the grass of the field, which is here today and tomorrow is thrown into the fire, will he not much more clothe you— you of little faith? So do not worry, saying, 'What shall we eat?' or 'What shall we drink?' or 'What shall we wear?' For the pagans run after all these things, and your heavenly Father knows that you need them.'

Where can I get more help?

- Go to page 66-71 for more information and recommended resources.

Written by Ems Hancock and Robin Rolls

What Would Jesus Tweet?
(Online Awareness)

?! **What's the issue?**

The internet is probably the most important invention in the last 100 years. It's changed the world as we know it and mostly for the better. The internet is not all good, neither is it all bad. We will take a look at some key topics and think about how we can respond.

Sharks, surfboards, and social media

The internet is a bit like the ocean…whether we're dipping our toes in the water, or swimming in the cool water; many of us love to be by the sea. The oceans of planet earth truly are beautiful but there's a darker side to the ocean too; great storms that can sink the biggest ships, waves that can wipe out a whole town, and thousands of predators searching for a tasty snack.

It's the same with the internet. It is amazing, and can be dangerous. You just need to know what to look out for. This issue contains some top tips on surfing the web without being eaten by sharks!

Risk, and the teenage brain.

Let's be honest; a life without risk is a boring life! There's a trick to knowing the difference between a good risk and one that has really bad consequences. Asking someone out on a date could be a good risk, but sending a naked selfie = bad risk!

You might know that your brain is currently under construction. No, seriously, it is! In fact, as a teenager, your brain will never again experience such massive change as is happening between your ears right now.

In the most basic terms it means that most of your decisions will be made on the basis of what feels good and not necessarily thinking about short or long term consequences. This feelings based part of our brains is called the amygdala. It helps us recognise pain, pleasure, and 'fight or flight' responses.

There are big changes in the cortex too. No, not the latest Nike trainers but the 'cortex'. It's the part of your brain that is home to your logic. This part of the brain helps us make good decisions, assess the long-term impact of our actions, recognise things that might be 'risky' and exercise self-control.

Because so much change is happening in the cortex, our brains at this time are more likely to push us to make decisions that feel good (using the amygdala) without fully taking in to account long term consequences.

Stuff is happening to your brain that will affect you for the rest of your life and that is so exciting! It also means that, if you make good decisions now, the consequences can stick for life. Use the adult brains around you and include their thoughts as you make decisions. They'll often be able to help you think about future consequences as well as what feels good now.

Want to know more about the brain? Check out the links on page 70.

Fill your mind with the good stuff! (Philippians 4:8-9)

Key issue 1: Immediacy

Our technology is with us all of the time. We're reachable 24 hours a day, 7 days a week and young people tell me they feel pressured to respond straight away from the moment they wake until the moment they fall asleep. Carla, a young person in a local school, told me "I just don't want to miss out".

This fear of missing out (FOMO) somehow makes us feel we have to always be available. But this can leave the people we're physically with fighting for scraps of our attention.

Responding immediately also has another disadvantage - very little time to think about our responses. Mistakes can be made when we rush into a comment or response, leading to feelings of regret later on.

One online survey said that 54% of people under 25 had posted something online they later regretted.

Some questions to think about:

- Who could you get advice from when responding to a difficult message online?
- I think some people spend so much time watching and reading about what others are up to that they're not fully living their own lives. What do you think?
- Do you ever feel like you're so busy connecting with people through technology that you forget to connect with the people in the room?

Top tip: Give yourself a break! When talking to a friend try putting your phone or tablet away until you've finished the conversation, you'll notice the difference!

In Matthew 6: 31-34 and 11: 28-30, Jesus invites his disciples to step away from the busyness and noise, stop worrying and get some rest. How can you take a rest from the noise of technology?

Key issue 2: Social Media

There are many great things about social media; it connects people across the world, enables instant anytime communication with friends and loved ones, to name just a few.

But we've all got Facebook friends who overshare with posts like "just off to the toilet" or post pointless things like "I'm bored. :-(". I often meet young people who find out the most intimate details and thoughts of friends online who never share that deeply face to face. (It can work just the same in the adult world too by the way).

Have you seen any of these examples of oversharing?

- Sharing hate or bullying messages
- Posting your every move including what you had for breakfast, lunch and dinner
- Sharing pictures of inappropriate situations, showing too much "skin", being with people or in places you shouldn't be
- Posting your home phone number or address
- Sharing online your fights with family or friends
- Posting personal information or pictures about your friends and family (especially without permission).

Perhaps we need to watch the words that flow out of our fingertips just as much as we watch the ones that come out of our mouths.

Top tip: When writing something or posting pictures online think about who could see it. If you wouldn't be happy for everyone to see it, don't write it, share it, like it, retweet it, tag it, or pin it.

I find it helpful to have a few people in mind, my mum, my boss, my best friends, and my girlfriend. If I'm ok with them seeing it, it's probably ok.

'Now we ask you, brothers and sisters, to acknowledge those who work hard among you, who care for you in the Lord and who admonish you. Hold them in the highest regard in love because of their work. Live in peace with each other. And we urge you, brothers and sisters, warn those who are idle and disruptive, encourage the disheartened, help the weak, be patient with everyone. Make sure that nobody pays back wrong for wrong, but always strive to do what is good for each other and for everyone else.

Rejoice always, pray continually, give thanks in all circumstances; for this is God's will for you in Christ Jesus.' 1 Thessalonians 5: 12-18.

If people had these verses in mind whilst talking online or posting a new status, what do you think would change?

Key issue 3: Sexting

If you're in secondary school, there's a good chance you've heard of sexting. It's where people send sexually explicit texts or photos to each other usually from one mobile device to another. My advice here is simple; don't do it.

If you're under 18, it's illegal to send a naked image of yourself to anyone and illegal to receive one - whether you asked for it or not.

From the Childline website:

Having sexting photos or videos on your phone or computer

If you are under the age of 18, the law sees you as a child. Therefore, if you have any indecent images or videos of somebody who is under 18 you would technically be in possession of an indecent image of a child – even if you are the same age. This is an offence under the Protection of Children Act 1978 and the Criminal Justice Act 1988.

Sending sexting photos or videos

If you are under 18 and you send, upload or forward indecent images or videos onto friends or boyfriends/girlfriends, this would also be breaking the law, even if they are photos of yourself ('selfies')

Earlier on I mentioned the brain. When someone finds you attractive your brain sends chemicals round our body that feel good! You might get butterflies, and nervous excitement. If they ask for a picture you might worry they'll reject you if you don't send it; that could feel bad. But... what are the long term implications?

You need to think about a whole range of things, not least the fact that when you send that image, not only is it illegal but you have absolutely no control over what happens to it, who it gets sent to, or how many times it gets sent. You also have no control over how it is used. It's a massive risk and one it's best to stay well away from. A bit of awkwardness over saying "no" to sexting is nothing compared to what happens when it goes wrong.

Top tip: If you're ever asked for a naked selfie, report it straight away. Tell your parents/carers, a youth worker, or a teacher. If you don't want to tell someone you know, you could call Childline on the number at the end of this booklet.

Already sent an image? Report it at www.ceop.police.uk/safety-centre

For more advice, see page 70.

'Desire without knowledge is not good - how much more will hasty feet miss the way!' Proverbs 19: 2.

You will make better decisions if you give yourself time, and get advice! What steps could you take to make good decisions in this area?

Have fun on the internet!

The internet is a thing of great opportunity, creativity, and fun. Technology is neither evil nor good but it can be used for both.

So go and have fun! Go and create, connect, and communicate! Share your ideas with others, stand up for those who can't stand up for themselves, crack jokes, share funny memories, tell inspiring stories, face fears and laugh. Represent our fun and creative God in the online space!

✚ Where can I get more help?

If you're ever concerned about anything that happens online, tell someone you can trust. Why not talk to a parent or carer, your youth worker or someone else you trust? They will be able to pray with you and give you advice and helpful tips. You can also contact:

CEOP

CEOP helps young people who are being sexually abused or are worried that someone they've met is trying to abuse them.

If you've met someone online, or face to face, and they are putting you under pressure to have sex or making you feel uncomfortable, you should report them to CEOP.

This might be someone:

- Making you have sex when you don't want to
- Chatting about sex online
- Asking you to meet up face to face if you've only met them online
- Asking you to do sexual things on webcam
- Asking for sexual pictures of you
- Making you feel worried, anxious or unsafe

If this is happening to you, or you're worried that it might be, report to: www.ceop.police.uk/safety-centre

Go to page 66-71 for more information and recommended resources.

Where Can I Get More Help?

Childline - 0800 11 11
www.childline.org.uk
help@nspcc.org.uk

NSPCC 0808 800 5000
www.nspcc.org.uk

Kidscape 020 7730 3300
www.kidscape.org.uk/young-people

The Samaritans 0845 790 90 90
www.samaritans.org

The Site
www.thesite.org

Youth Access 0208 7729900
www.youthaccess.org.uk

CEOP
www.ceop.police.uk/safety-centre

You may find it helpful to use creative websites such as au.reachout.com
an Australian website with lots of useful advice.

FOR MORE DETAIL ON SOME OF THESE ISSUES:

?! God & Spiritual Things

NEW LIFE/GUIDANCE
www.cwr.org.uk
www.christianityexplored.org
www.alpha.org

FORGIVENESS
www.theforgivennessproject.com

OCCULT
The Reachout Trust - 0870 770 3258
Offers advice from a Christian perspective
www.reachouttrust.org

DOMESTIC ABUSE

All children and young people have equal rights and the right to live a healthy, happy and fulfilling life. The UN Convention on the Rights of the Child (UNRC) has been signed by 197 countries, including the UK. This lists all the rights that children and young people have. These beliefs underpin your rights: you have the right to be protected and live free from violence, abuse or harm.

www.restoredrelationships.org
www.thehideout.org.uk
thisisabuse.direct.gov.uk
www.safetotalk.org.uk/professionals/supporting-children-living-with-domestic-violence-and-abuse
www.barnardos.org.uk/what_we_do/our_work/domestic_violence.htm
www.womensaid.org.uk

QUESTIONING YOUR SEXUALITY

Inclusive Church - inclusive-church.com
Are committed to working towards the church being open and welcome to all people.
The site has an online directory of inclusive churches so you can find one near you.

Diverse Church - diversechurch.org.uk
An online community of 18 – 30yr olds who identify as 'Fully LGBT and Fully Christian' Although a closed group they regularly post podcasts and youtube videos that anyone of any age can access.

Living Out - www.livingout.org

The Gay Christian Network - www.gaychristian.net

WATCH WHAT YOU WATCH (PORNOGRAPHY)

XXXchurch (xxxchurch.com/teens) offers online help.
dirtygirlsministries.com

The Naked Truth campaign (nakedtruthproject.com) aims to open eyes and free lives from the negative effects of porn.

Internet accountability and porn filters:
Covenant Eyes (covenanteyes.com) monitors the content of web pages you have viewed, and sends it to someone you choose (maybe a youth leader).
X3watch (x3watch.com) monitors the content of web pages and can also block access.

SEX

www.romanceacademy.org
www.relationshipdilemma.com
www.todayschristianwoman.com

?! Doing Life

ADDICTIONS

Drinkline - 0800 7 314 314
www.drinksmarter.org

Quit - 0800 00 22 00
www.quit.org.uk

Frank - 0300 123 6600 or text 82111
www.talktofrank.com

BEREAVEMENT

www.winstonswish.org.uk
www.rd4u.org.uk

BULLYING

www.bullying.co.uk
www.beatbullying.org
www.youngminds.org/Bullying
www.kidscape.org.uk

DEPRESSION

Careline - 0208 514 1177

Young Minds - 0207 336 8445
www.youngminds.org.uk

Mind - 0300 123 3393
www.mind.org.uk

EATING DISORDERS

www.anorexiabulimiacare.org.uk
www.b-eat.co.uk
www.foundationsuk.org

LIVING AN ETHICAL LIFE

www.tearfund.org/en/about_you/campaign
www.tearfund.org/en/about_you/youth
www.ethicalconsumer.org
www.fairtrade.org.uk

LONELINESS

www.wikihow.com/Deal-With-Loneliness
www.soon.org.uk
www.getconnected.org.uk/get_help/feelings_and_mental_health/emotional_problems

SELF HARM

www.selfharm.co.uk
www.thesite.org/mental-health/self-harm

WHAT WOULD JESUS TWEET?
(ONLINE AWARENESS)

www.thinkuknow.co.uk/14_plus/need-advice/selfies-and-sexting
www.saferinternet.org.uk/ufiles/so-you-got-naked-online.pdf

The Brain - Want to know more about the brain?
www.youtube.com/watch?v=hiduiTq1ei8
www.youtube.com/watch?v=f9Ya0mHsIgM
www.youtube.com/watch?v=LWUkW4s3XxY (view from a university professor)

📖 Recommended Books

NEW LIFE/GUIDANCE
Counterfeit Gods - Timothy Keller
Just Do Something - Kevin DeYoung
One Life: What's It All About? - Rico Tice And Barry Cooper

A LIFE CHANGING STORY
Honest Evangelism - Rico Tice and Carl Laferton

LIVE LIFE TO THE MAX
Generous Justice - Timothy Keller

FORGIVENESS
God Meant It For Good - R T Kendall
Total Forgiveness - R T Kendall

HOLY SPIRIT
Spirit Filled Church - Terry Virgo
Forgotten God - Francis Chan
Encounter The Holy Spirit - Jeannie Morgan

DOMESTIC ABUSE
Beauty For Ashes - Joyce Meyer

FAMILY
A Loving Life - Paul Miller

QUESTIONING YOUR SEXUALITY
Love Is An Orientation - Andrew Marin
Dazzling Darkness - Rachel Mann
Washed And Waiting - Wesley Hill
Gay And Catholic - Eve Tushnet

SEX
Passion And Purity: Learning To Bring Your Love Life Under Christ's Control - Elizabeth Elliot
Sex Is Not The Problem (Lust Is) - Joshua Harris

WATCH WHAT YOU WATCH (PORNOGRAPHY)
Proven Men - Joel Hesch
Every Young Man's Battle - Steven Arterburn and Fred Stoeker
Every Young Woman's Battle - Shannon Ethridge and Stephen Arteburn
No Stones: Women Redeemed From Sexual Addiction - Marnie C Ferree

DEPRESSION/LONELINESS
God Will Use This For Good - Max Lucado
God Knows My Name - Beth Redman
The Ragamuffin-Gospel - Brennan Manning

EATING DISORDERS
Eating Disorders - Dr K. Middleton
Beyond Chaotic Eating - Helena Wilkinson
Hidden Hunger - Maxine Vorster
A New Name - Emma Scrivener

LIVING AN ETHICAL LIFE
Irresistible Revolution - Shane Claiborne
Lift the Label - David Westlake & Esther Stansfield
L is for Lifestyle - Ruth Valerio
God of the Poor - Dewi Hughes
Bonfire of the Brands - Neil Boorman
Actions Speak Louder - Tearfund

SELF IMAGE
Compared To Her - Sophie de Witt